D-DAY

WORLD

TURNING POINTS OF

WAR II

D-DAY

MILTON DANK

A GROLIER COMPANY

FRANKLIN WATTS ■ 1984
NEW YORK ■ LONDON ■ TORONTO ■ SYDNEY

Photographs courtesy of:
UPI: pp. 9, 15, 62, 77, 86, 99, 100;
U.S. Army: pp. 35, 38, 69;
U.S. Air Force: p. 44;
Imperial War Museum: p. 56;
Culver Pictures Inc.: pp. 28, 80, 89.

Maps courtesy of Vantage Art, Inc.

Library of Congress Cataloging in Publication Data
D-Day.
(Turning points of World War II)
Includes index.
Summary: Traces the events of Operation Overlord,
the Allied invasion of German-occupied France from the
beaches of Normandy, which took place on June 6, 1944.
1. World War, 1939-1945—Campaigns—France—
Normandy—Juvenile literature.   2. Operation Overlord
—Juvenile literature   3. Normandy (France)—History
—Juvenile literature.   [1. World War, 1939-1945—
Campaigns—France—Normandy.   2. Operation Overlord.
3. Normandy (France)—History]   I. Title.   II. Series.
D756.5.N6D3 1984   940.54'21   84-7326
ISBN 0-531-04863-2

CONTENTS

CHAPTER

D-DAY: A TURNING POINT IN WORLD WAR II

By the beginning of 1944, the Second World War had lasted almost four and a half years. When Germany invaded Poland on September 1, 1939, no one dreamed that the war could last so long. Great Britain and France had declared war on Nazi Germany confident that the French army and the British navy would soon bring Hitler to his knees.

The first three years of the war were an almost unbroken series of Nazi victories. Using massed tanks and planes in a new strategy called "lightning war" (*blitzkrieg*), the German armies crushed Poland while the Allies sat without attacking behind the fortifications of the Maginot Line. This string of forts along the French–German border (but not along the French–Belgian frontier) gave them a feeling of security. The Allies felt they could avoid the terrible slaughter of the First World War by holding the Maginot Line and allowing a naval blockade to starve Germany into submission. It was a futile plan.

While England and France waited, Hitler sent his armies into Norway and Denmark, claiming the Allies had intended to land there. He used this period of "Phoney War" to build up his armed strength for the decisive attack on France.

This massive assault came on the morning of May 10, 1940 as the German troops plunged into Belgium, Holland, and

Luxemburg. It looked at first like a repeat of the German attack in 1914, and the best French and British divisions rushed into Belgium to repel the invaders. But the Germans were not about to repeat the mistakes of Kaiser Wilhelm II. When the Allies were committed to defending Belgium, the main German attack came at Sedan in France where the Maginot Line ended. The blitzkrieg crushed the French armies holding this critical point and sent Nazi panzer divisions racing to the English Channel to cut off the Allied armies in Belgium. It was a complete and total victory. Surrounded, the small Belgian and Dutch armies were forced to surrender. The British and French troops were slowly pushed back toward Dunkirk on the Channel. There, under constant attack by tanks and planes, over 335,000 Allied soldiers were taken off the beaches and returned to England. Behind them they left all their heavy guns, tanks, and other equipment. Still, it was a miracle that they escaped, the "miracle of Dunkirk."

Unable to withstand the Nazi blitzkrieg, France surrendered after six weeks of fighting. Under an aged hero of the First World War, Marshal Henri Philippe Pétain, the French government signed a humiliating armistice with Germany and Italy (eager to share in the spoils, Mussolini had declared war on the Allies just before the French surrender). The Nazis occupied most of France including the Atlantic coast down to Spain, and forced the weak French government to pay a staggering daily cost for maintaining the German occupation army.

Alone on her island, her army without heavy weapons, facing the formidable German air force, England seemed on the verge of defeat. The "Battle of Britain" began as the German planes began constant air raids intended to force the British to surrender. The Royal Air Force fought gallantly but was on the brink of losing the critical air battle when Hitler made a mistake. Because German cities had been bombed by the RAF, he ordered London destroyed. This switch saved the RAF airfields from destruction and finally won the Battle of Britain. Although London and other English cities suffered horribly and over 20,000 civilians were killed, the RAF grew in strength and finally dominated the air over England.

Hitler had planned an invasion of the British Isles (Operation Sea Lion), but with the RAF and Britain's Royal Navy still undefeated, he was forced to cancel it. Furious at his failure to crush England, he made his second great mistake. On June 22, 1941, he sent his armies against the Soviet Union despite the treaty of friendship he had signed with Stalin in 1939. With England still in the war, Hitler had opened up a second front, the great fear of German military planners.

At first it looked like another tremendous Nazi victory march. Hitler's armies smashed through disorganized Russian resistance, taking more than a million prisoners and rolling within sight of Moscow. But winter came early that year in Russia and the German tanks and trucks were stalled in the snow and ice of the endless Russian plains. The Soviet general staff took advantage of the bad weather and great distances, pulling their soldiers back and refusing battle until their Siberian armies could arrive. By the end of 1941, it was a stalemate.

Then came Pearl Harbor. The Japanese surprise air raid crippled the U.S. Navy and allowed the Japanese to capture the Philippines, Malaya, Guam, and such important bases as Singapore and Hong Kong. Unopposed, the Japanese swept through U.S., British, Dutch, and French possessions in the South Pacific. It was another blitzkrieg, a naval one.

Japan was allied to Germany and Italy by the "Pact of Steel" that required the other two partners to aid the third if it were attacked. Since Japan had started the war against the United States, Hitler and Mussolini could have refused to help her, but Hitler was at the peak of his success. Overconfident about the war in Russia, he declared war on the United States and forced Italy to do the same. This was his third great mistake, for it is doubtful that the United States, fully engaged in the Pacific, would have enlarged the war by fighting Germany and Italy at the same time. With this larger war forced on her, the United States girded for the coming battles.

It would be a global war, fought in the steaming jungles of Pacific islands, on the sands of the North African desert, in the olive groves of Sicily and Italy, and finally in the fields of northwest Europe and the air over Japan. No one has ever counted how many men, women, and children died in this titanic struggle. The best figure is fifty million. The number of wounded and missing will never be known.

On one side was Nazi Germany and its allies: Italy, Japan, and "friendly neutrals" like Spain, Finland, Rumania, Hungary, France, and other countries that sent soldiers to fight only the Russians. On the other side were the United States, the Soviet Union, Britain and its dominions, plus the tiny forces of the "governments in exile" of Free France, Holland, Belgium, Poland, Czechoslovakia, Norway, and others. The first part of the war had all gone Hitler's way, but now, slowly, it began to change.

The alliance between the United States and Great Britain dominated the war effort outside of the Soviet Union. Since these two countries would bear the brunt of the fighting and supply most of the soldiers and money needed to defeat the enemy, they controlled the strategy. Alliances in war are notoriously weak, divided by different national interests, power struggles, jealousy, and personal dislikes. All these would show up in the united war effort of the United States and Britain, but the amazing thing was that these differences were never allowed to sway their resolve to win the war. Time and again national interests were set aside, struggles for high command generously resolved, jealousies suppressed, and personal antagonisms sternly put down. Napoleon, who knew the weaknesses of combinations of his enemies, once said, "May I always fight against allies!" Hitler would not be as lucky, although he hoped to the end for divisions among his foes.

The chain of command in the Allied war effort was kept

simple. The U.S. and British chiefs of staff met and laid out the military strategy options that their strengths allowed. President Franklin D. Roosevelt and the British prime minister, Winston S. Churchill, meeting in Quebec, Casablanca, or at Yalta with Stalin, would approve or disapprove these plans. Changed and revised, the plans then led to orders to the commanders in the field. One of the first decisions to be made was the agreement to defeat Germany first and fight a holding action in the Pacific until Hitler fell. One can imagine the anguish this decision caused to the Allied commanders in the Pacific.

The tide of battle began to turn in the Allies' favor in November 1942. American and British soldiers landed in North Africa, occupying the French colonies of Morocco and Algeria after stiff resistance from French troops loyal to the Nazi-leaning government of Marshal Pétain. In Egypt, Hitler's favorite general, Field Marshal Erwin Rommel, the ever-victorious "Desert Fox," was defeated at El Alamein by the British Eighth Army under General Bernard L. Montgomery.

It took six months of severe fighting, including a U.S. defeat at Kasserine Pass, before Rommel was trapped between the two armies in Tunisia. Hitler ordered his favorite general back to Berlin, not wanting him to be captured with the rest of his Afrika Korps. In July, the Allies landed in Sicily, quickly cleared the island, and swept on into Italy. Mussolini fell and Italy sued for an armistice. The Nazis occupied the northern mountains of Italy and prepared to hold them to the end. Further Allied landings at Anzio and Salerno failed to push the Germans out of their mountain strongholds. Again it was a stalemate.

By the end of 1943, Hitler held the landmass of Europe, with the Anglo-American armies hitting him from the south and the Soviet armies striking from the east. Although the Germans had lost a whole army of 300,000 men in the surrender at Stalingrad, there were still over two million Nazi soldiers facing the Red Army. Russian losses in two years had been staggering, and Marshal Stalin was sternly demanding a "Second Front"—an Allied landing in France that would force Hitler to move some of his divisions from the Eastern Front. There was an implied Soviet threat that if the Anglo-Americans failed to attack—or did not succeed in the attack—Russia would have to sign a negotiated peace with Hitler to avoid further devastation. There was a great lack of trust between the British and Americans on one side and the Soviets on the other. The Russians were convinced that the Anglo-Americans were willing to let Hitler and Stalin bleed each other to death while doing nothing to help their Soviet ally.

Fearful that Russia might leave the war, the United States and Great Britain did what they could to reassure the suspicious Stalin. As early as August 1942, France's Channel port of Dieppe was raided by Canadian soldiers and British commandos. The attack was a disaster. The alert German troops killed, wounded, or captured over half the landing force of five thousand men. It was clear that a German-defended port could not be taken by a surprise attack.

In the meetings of the Allied Combined Chiefs of Staff in Washington, D.C., the problem of a landing in France was argued, often hotly, for two years. Led by the U.S. Army chief of staff, General George C. Marshall, the Americans were strongly in favor of invading Europe at the earliest opportunity. The British were reluctant, fearful of the terrible casualties that might result and the consequences of a failure to secure a beachhead on the continent.

If the invasion failed, it would be years before the Allies could assemble the men and equipment to try again. Stalin might sign a separate peace. Hitler might have time to get his new weapons—the rockets, the jet fighters, the new submarines, even the atomic bomb—and swiftly win the war. The whole outcome of the Second World War might depend on the success or failure of the invasion of France.

In August 1943, Roosevelt and Churchill met in Quebec, Canada, and approved the idea of the invasion. Planning now began in earnest, with a target date for the landings set for early May 1944. General Dwight D. Eisenhower, Allied commander in North Africa, was selected to lead the Anglo-American forces in the invasion. The great enterprise was given the code name "Operation Overlord." This plan covered not only landing the Allied armies on the coast of France but the battles that would follow on the road to Berlin. The crossing of the Channel and establishing a beachhead on the French coast was the first and crucial step.

While stupendous quantities of war matériel were shipped across the Atlantic through the German submarine blockade, or poured from the British factories, the Overlord planners examined their maps, weighed the weather, the tides, the beaches, and made a thousand calculations to determine where the invasion was most likely to succeed. It had to be within the range of fighter planes so that the troops struggling ashore would have aerial protection, but most of all, there had to be surprise.

The shortest route for a Channel crossing was from Dover to Calais (see map, page 16). This, however, was where the Germans would expect the invasion, and it was the most heavily fortified part of the French coast. Finally the Allied planners turned their eyes to the lush, hedgerowed fields of Normandy.

The crossing would take more than twice as long as Dover-Calais, but the fighters could cover it. The beaches were suitable and, most important, the large port of Cherbourg could be attacked and captured from the land side. The seizure of a large port was vital for the landing of the huge quantities of supplies needed to maintain the Allied armies in the field.

These landing craft carry
British and Canadian troops
back to their destroyer after
the unsuccessful Dieppe raid.

After months of planning, the decision was made to postpone the invasion until the first week of June to allow more supplies to reach England. Training of the troops continued at an increasing pace. The Allied air forces bombed key bridges, roads, and railroad yards to isolate the invasion area and also to convince the Germans that Calais was the target. By the middle of May 1944, the vast machinery of Operation Overlord was rolling at high speed. Now the Allied commanders met for the last time to go over their plans and to make certain that nothing had been left to chance. They knew that for any mistake or oversight, men would die and the war could be lost.

CHAPTER

THE
OVERLORD
PLAN

Monday, May 15, 1944. St. Paul's School, a Victorian Gothic building in West London, was the scene of the final review of Operation Overlord, the invasion of Normandy. The school was the headquarters of General Bernard Montgomery's 21st Army Group and Montgomery would command all the Allied ground forces. In the halls that had once been filled with chattering schoolboys, the men responsible for the mightest air and sea assault the world had ever seen gathered to go over the plans once more.

As they found their seats in the two-tiered circular lecture hall, the main actors in the front rows on the lower floor and the bit players in the packed gallery, there was an air of nervous anticipation. No one needed to be reminded of what was at stake in this assault. Victory over Hitler's Germany or what was unthinkable—defeat—might well depend on how well Overlord had been planned and how successfully it was carried out. If the Nazis knew where the landings would take place, the Allied armies would be slaughtered on the beaches. A repulse like that could spell the end of the Allied attempts to strike at Germany through France. It would be years before another force as large as the one now straining at the leash here in England could again be assembled.

The curved narrow benches intended for squirming

boys must have been uncomfortable for the senior officers in their immaculate uniforms adorned with the bright-colored ribbons of their medals. Those in the gallery looked down at the front row of seats where King George VI and the British prime minister, Winston Churchill, sat next to the Supreme Commander, Allied Expeditionary Force, General Dwight D. Eisenhower. Beside them sat Montgomery, who would lead the ground troops, and the commanders of the air forces and the navy in this awesome enterprise.

Everyone who had a significant role in Overlord was present. With a shiver, one of the naval officers wondered what would happen if the Germans had gotten word of this review and sent bombers to level St. Paul's School. Or if flying unmanned bombs—the "buzz bombs" that intelligence had warned them of—were even now speeding across the Channel toward this building.

"The first to rise and break the silence was the Supreme Commander himself," wrote a U.S. naval officer. "It had been said that his smile was worth twenty divisions. That day it was worth more. He spoke for ten minutes. Before the warmth of his quiet confidence the mists of doubt dissolved. When he was finished the tension was gone. Not often has one man been called upon to accept so great a burden of responsibility."

Inspiring confidence in this "Great Crusade" was Eisenhower's main task—that and keeping unity in the Anglo-American alliance. There were many strains, antagonisms, and disagreements between the senior British and American officers. Led by Churchill, the British had fought for over two years against a cross-Channel invasion. Time and again in the meetings of the combined staffs, they had warned of the risk of a bloody repulse that could mean losing or certainly prolonging the war. Britain had been fighting for almost five years, the whole country had suffered from air raids and defeats. The manpower barrel was empty. If Overlord failed, there might have to be a negotiated peace that would leave Nazi Germany with most of its conquests in Europe.

Almost all of the British officers present that day had served as young men in the frightful bloodletting of the First World War and that awful experience had scarred their minds. At any cost they were determined to avoid throwing masses of men against an entrenched enemy sitting in fortified positions. Monty (as Montgomery was known) himself had been shot through the chest in France in 1914. At the field dressing station, the doctors gave him up as dying and his grave was dug. But the stubborn young lieutenant refused to die. He survived to serve as a division commander in World War II, went through the hell of Dunkirk, and brilliantly led the British Eighth Army to victory in North Africa over the man who would oppose him in France, Field Marshal Erwin Rommel.

When Eisenhower finished talking, it was Monty's turn. A born actor with a love for being the center of attention, he clearly enjoyed performing for this distinguished audience. Standing in front of a huge map of the Channel coast, he explained how his 21st Army Group would assault the Normandy beaches, fight their way inland after cracking the German fortifications, then break out into the open country in a headlong dash for the German frontier. He left no doubt in the minds of his listeners that he expected Overlord to be an overwhelming success.

The plan had been over two years in the making. It was a massive, complicated project that required thousands of pages just to outline. It needed such delicate coordination and timing of whole armies plus so many thousands of planes and ships that some of the men in the room felt that only the hand of God could make it work. A failure at any one of a hundred points would throw the whole finely balanced plan into chaos. Nothing like this had ever been attempted before: on D-Day, eight divisions—say, eighty thousand men—would be the first assault wave. Three of the divisions—one British and two U.S.—would be airborne, paratroopers and glider troops that would drop from the skies during the night to seize certain vital points. At dawn, five infantry divisions

General Dwight D. Eisenhower confers
with Britain's General Bernard Montgomery,
who was promoted to the rank of
field marshal after the Normandy invasion.

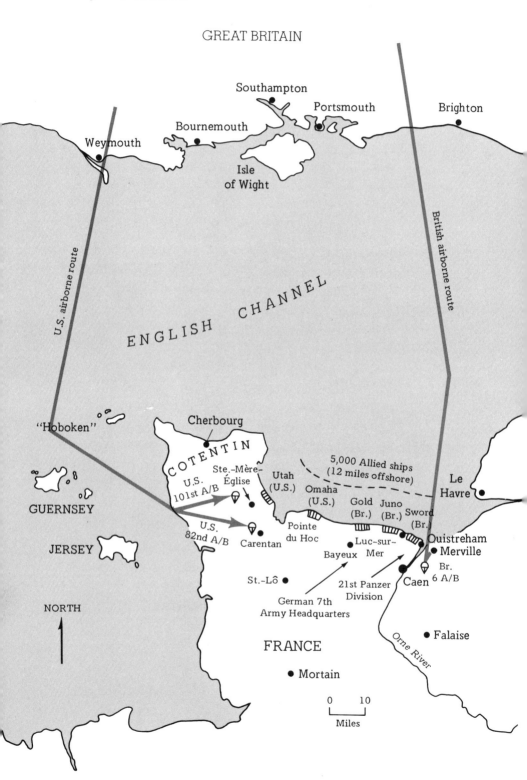

OPERATION OVERLORD
June 6, 1944

GREAT BRITAIN

Southampton

Portsmouth

Brighton

Bournemouth

Weymouth

Isle
of Wight

U.S. airborne route

British airborne route

ENGLISH CHANNEL

"Hoboken"

Cherbourg

COTENTIN

Ste.-Mère-
Église

U.S.
101st A/B

Utah
(U.S.)

5,000 Allied ships
(12 miles offshore)

Omaha
(U.S.)

Gold
(Br.)

Juno
(Br.)

Sword
(Br.)

Le
Havre

GUERNSEY

U.S.
82nd A/B

Carentan

Pointe
du Hoc

Luc-sur-
Mer

Ouistreham
Merville

JERSEY

Bayeux

St.-Lô

21st Panzer
Division

Br.
6 A/B

Caen

NORTH

German 7th
Army Headquarters

Falaise

Orne River

FRANCE

Mortain

0   10

Miles

would begin landing on five beaches stretching from the east coast of the Cotentin Peninsula to the mouth of the Orne River (see map, page 16).

After the German fortifications, the so-called "Atlantic Wall," had been broken by the initial assault and a firm beachhead established, divisions would be poured in rapidly. In three months, there would be thirty-nine Allied divisions in Normandy. Once the German armies in France were broken, the Allied forces would begin a drive for the heart of Germany itself.

But first the Allies had to establish themselves firmly on an impregnable beachhead, turn back the inevitable counterattack by strong German panzer divisions, and finally break out into the open country. To build up the strength in men, guns, and tanks quickly meant that a port, a harbor capable of handling large ships, would have to be seized immediately. One reason the Cotentin Peninsula of Normandy had been selected for the landings was the presence of Cherbourg, a major harbor at its northern tip. The U.S. troops landing at Utah Beach at the base of the peninsula would drive straight across the Cotentin, isolate the area from counterattack, and capture Cherbourg. Until this port was taken, all the reinforcements and mountains of supplies would have to come over the open invasion beaches. They would be subject to attack by guns, planes, and even "buzz bombs."

To protect the ships offloading at the beaches from the storms for which the Channel was notorious, old merchant ships would be sunk in a continuous line to create an artificial breakwater. As an outer seawall, huge concrete boxes would be towed across the Channel and sunk in place. These artificial harbors, called "Mulberries," were as high as three-story buildings and designing them to stand the strong tides of the Normandy coast was a major accomplishment. Additional ships would be sunk off each of the beaches to form a shelter for landing craft since only two "Mulberries" were planned. Gasoline for the thousands of vehicles that would swarm over the beaches would be pumped through "Pluto," a pipeline that would be laid under the sea from England to Normandy. This had to be done, for a gasoline-filled tanker unloading off the beaches was too vulnerable to enemy attack.

When Monty was finished, the commander of the invasion sea forces, the British Admiral Sir Bertram Ramsay, spoke. He would be responsible for the five thousand ships that would carry the assault troops across the Channel, bombard the enemy defenses that threatened the beaches, then send the troops in on landing craft. Never before in history had such a fleet been assembled. Coordination and timing of all these warships was a headache that had given him many sleepless nights. What would the weather be? Would his ships have to fight high waves and poor visibility, both of which would mean inaccurate gunfire on enemy positions? Admiral Ramsay was an old sea dog and he could remember his naval history. In 1915, a British fleet had bombarded Turkish guns and strong points on the Gallipoli peninsula. Then British troops had been landed on the beaches by small landing craft in the face of strong Turkish gunfire. Nine months later, after futile fighting, the British expeditionary force had to be evacuated. There had been over a quarter of a million casualties in this futile attempt to seize the Dardanelles and Constantinople. There were many men in the room today who as young officers had gone through the hell of Gallipoli. It was a lesson they could not forget.

Air Chief Marshal Sir Trevor Leigh-Mallory had been a flier in the First World War and had commanded fighters in the Battle of Britain. Now he commanded all the Allied air forces: fighters, bombers, and transport planes. For months now, bombers had ranged over northwest France, blowing up bridges, railroad yards, German gun positions near the invasion beaches, and any other target that was a threat to Overlord. In order to hide where the actual landings would take place, as many bombs were dropped in the Pas de Calais, the nearest French territory to England, as in Normandy. It was in Calais, just thirty sea miles (55 km) from Dover, England, that the Germans expected the Allied invasion to take place. It was here that they kept the bulk of their armies, including the powerful panzer divisions. Hitler had worried about Normandy and had ordered it reinforced, but he still thought that any landing there would be a diversion and that the Allies would take the shortest route across the Channel and the one closest to the German border. Leigh-Mallory's bombers had hit the Pas de Calais hard to encourage this belief. Meanwhile, bridges, roads, and railroads leading to Normandy had been blasted.

But there was another part of the Overlord plan that worried Leigh-Mallory. Hours before the seaborne assault, 16,000 U.S. and 8,000 British paratroopers and glider forces would drop into Normandy to seize vital points like the causeways over flooded ground that were the only exits from Utah Beach. This was the assigned task of the U.S. 101st Airborne Division which, with the 82nd Airborne, made up the U.S. paratroop force.

In the night, unarmed and unarmored transport planes carrying the airborne force would have to fly at low altitude across the Cotentin Peninsula from the west coast to the east. There would be a steady stream of over a thousand planes, each carrying about twenty paratroopers or towing a glider. Made of steel tubing and canvas or of oak ribs and plywood, the motorless craft were essential to the airborne assault. The paratroopers jumped with only the weapons they could carry on their bodies. Landing in small fields, the gliders would bring in jeeps, cannon, antitank guns, radios, land mines, and extra ammunition. They also carried the glider infantry and artillery regiment of the division. What the paratroopers feared most was a German tank counterattack early in the operation. To repel this, the guns that only the gliders could bring in were vital.

Leigh-Mallory worried about the vulnerability of this constant stream of slow (140 mph [224 kph]) twin-engined planes flying only a thousand feet above the ground. He thought that the alerted German antiaircraft guns would take a terrible toll of them. He warned Eisenhower that three quarters of these troops would never survive the flight. It would be a slaughter of two fine divisions.

This was just one of the headaches that the Supreme Commander had to face. Only he could decide whether Leigh-Mallory was correct. Could he afford to ignore the terrible warning given by his air forces commander?

One U.S. general, Omar Bradley, insisted that the landings on Utah would be in grave peril unless the causeways were taken by the airborne. There was no other way to get off the beach. The U.S. airborne commanders, Major General Matthew Ridgway of the 82nd and Major General Maxwell Taylor of the 101st, disagreed strongly with Leigh-Mallory's estimate of their expected losses. True, they admitted, the airborne assault in Sicily almost a year ago had been badly bungled, but they had since learned a lot about parachuting and gliding troops at night.

Eisenhower alone had to reach a decision. Without the airborne, Utah was in grave danger. A failure at Utah would put Omaha Beach and the British beaches in peril. Overlord could fail if the causeways were not taken. So the airborne would have to take their chances. After all, Leigh-Mallory's grim prediction was only a guess with which the senior airborne commanders disagreed. The decision was made: the U.S. airborne divisions would have to go in and take their chances.

Leigh-Mallory said nothing of his fears at the review. The decision had been made and the responsibility was Eisenhower's. He finished his talk by pointing out the Allied air superiority over the German Luftwaffe and promising it would be maintained over the landing beaches.

After lunch the king, George VI, spoke briefly, fighting to overcome his stammer. There were other talks by senior commanders about the role of their forces in Overlord. Then Winston Churchill, the British prime minister, rose to speak last.

Everyone in the room knew how long and how hard Churchill had fought against the cross-Channel attack. In his meetings with President Roosevelt, he had urged an advance "through the soft underbelly" of Nazi Europe, that is through Italy and the Balkans. This would satisfy Stalin's demand for a Second Front to draw off German troops from Russia and would strike Hitler where he was weakest. Every time an obstacle to Overlord, such as the shortage of landing craft, had come up, Churchill had pushed for the postponement if not the abandonment of Overlord. All his arguments had been countered by Eisenhower and General Marshall, who was not only the U.S. Army chief of staff but President Roosevelt's valued advisor. To get the needed landing craft, the invasion of southern France that had been planned to take place at the same time as Overlord was postponed for a month and the needed craft sent to England. Also, the date of the Normandy attack was moved from the beginning of May to the beginning of June so that another month's production of landing craft would be available.

It was the memory of Gallipoli that made Churchill anxious. That campaign had been his idea as a young cabinet minister—First Lord of the Admiralty. He had pushed that idea and had gotten it approved despite the objections of senior officers. The failure at Gallipoli had forced Churchill to resign from the government. He had gone to fight in the trenches of the Western Front, saddened by the terrible loss of life in this attempt to capture Constantinople. If Overlord failed, it would be another Gallipoli.

Still, he had been heartened by what he had heard of the plans and the landings were now inevitable. He started off quietly but built up to a fighting finish with the words, "Gentlemen, I am hardening to this enterprise!"

The review ended on this note. Now nothing was left to do but to set the date, the exact day, for this great "enterprise."

D-Day depended on many factors. The shortage of landing craft had forced a postponement until the beginning of June. The navy wanted the tide to be low so that the obstacles the Germans had planted in the water would be exposed and could be destroyed. But they needed a rising tide shortly thereafter so that the landing craft could float over any obstacles left. The warships needed light enough to see their targets for the initial bombardment and an onshore wind to clear the smoke from the explosion of the shells.

The airborne would be going in in the dark but they needed moonlight to minimize injuries on landing, no clouds at the altitude the planes would use, and light winds so that the parachutists would not be dragged or the gliders blown aside on landing.

The army assault troops needed all this and small wave heights so that the landing craft could maneuver easily and the amphibious tanks with their inflatable belts would not be swamped and sink.

The tide and moon conditions would be met during the period from June 5 to 7. The weather, of course, could not be predicted with any accuracy until three or four days in advance, but it was decided that if the weather was suitable, Overlord would begin on the morning of June 5. This allowed a postponement for a maximum of forty-eight hours if the weather was bad on the fifth. No one wanted to even think of what might happen if the invasion had to be put off until the next tide and moon period two weeks later. Only a very few senior officers knew the date of D-Day, but by June 5 a hundred thousand men would know that Normandy was the landing place. How could such a secret be kept from the Germans for two weeks? Since the beginning of 1944, security had been a very difficult operation.

Elaborate schemes to convince the Germans that the invasion would hit the Pas de Calais had been put into operation. Early in the war, British intelligence had captured every German agent in England. A number of these had been "turned," agreeing to work for the Allies. For a long time the credibility of certain of these double agents had been built up by allowing them to send what seemed to be valuable information—supplied of course by British intelligence. As D-Day approached, these agents transmitted reports that seemed to indicate a landing in the Pas de Calais. Unaware that these agents had been "turned," German officers in Berlin believed these reports.

In southeast England, opposite the Pas de Calais, a U.S. Army group seemed to be poised to strike across the Channel. Headquarters buildings were erected, airfields built, tanks parked nearby, even radio messages sent from the "First U.S. Army Group." Lieutenant General George S. Patton, Jr., was rumored to be the commanding officer, and his arrival in England was leaked to the press. The double agents reported this buildup and German reconnaissance planes confirmed it, but the aerial photos failed to show that the tanks, trucks, planes and other equipment were built of paper, wood, and rubber. It was deception on a grand scale.

In the battle of intelligence, the Allies were clear winners. Just before the war began, the British obtained a prototype of the Ultra coding machine used by the German Army. This enabled them to read messages from Hitler and German Army headquarters to their commanders in the field. The Japanese code had been broken by U.S. Navy Intelligence and reports by the Japanese ambassador to Berlin on his tour of the German fortifications on the French coast were very valuable in planning Overlord.

But security is more than cracking enemy codes and the other triumphs of intelligence services. There were failures, too, mostly human failures. A U.S. Air Force general made an indiscreet reference to the date of Overlord at a cocktail party in a London hotel. Although he was a West Point classmate of General Eisenhower, the general was quickly sent back to the States and reduced to his permanent rank of lieutenant colonel. In another error, an army postal clerk accidentally mailed a package of Overlord reports to his sister in Chicago instead of the gift he had intended. The package broke apart in the Chicago post office and the strange reports were turned over to the FBI. Other Overlord reports blew out of an office window in London and were quickly gathered by a passerby who then disappeared after handing them back to a sentry.

A Czech officer named Miksche serving with the Free French Army had published a book in 1943 about the future of airborne operations in war. As an example of tactics, he described an airborne attack on Normandy to support a seaborne landing. By an amazing coincidence, the landing areas he suggested were almost exactly those the Allied airborne would use, and the beach for the seaborne attack was exactly where Utah Beach was. Miksche even had the number of airborne divisions correct: three. Had the Germans seen this book? If they had, did they now believe that Normandy would be the main invasion spot?

What were the German commanders thinking? What were their plans for repulsing the invasion?

HITLER
PREPARES
FOR
INVASION

The art of war, an English historian once said, was nothing more than guessing what was going on on the "other side of the hill." The Allies tried to guess the German plans, and their enemy tried to foresee where and when the invasion would come. Both tried to deceive the other.

Hitler's choice to command his armies against Overlord was a sixty-nine-year-old aristocrat of the old school. Field Marshal Gerd von Rundstedt was called "the last Prussian" by his respectful juniors. He was a stiff, unyielding man who had never lost a campaign. He had directed the victorious blitzkrieg that had crushed France, Holland, and Belgium in six weeks. Sent to Russia as an army commander, he had been outspoken in his criticisms of Hitler's strategy there until finally the Fuehrer had forced him into retirement. Early in 1942, he had been called back as Commander in Chief, West. Von Rundstedt quickly learned that he had been given an impossible job.

First of all, the field marshal had to defend three thousand miles (4,800 km) of coastline, from the German border in the north all the way to the Italian frontier. For this crushing task, he had been given some sixty divisions, few of them first-rate. For a long time, France had been treated as a resting center for troops that had suffered heavy losses on the

Russian front. With German manpower dangerously low, their ranks had been filled out with Soviet prisoners of war, men who had been given the choice of starving to death in P.O.W. camps or putting on German uniforms. Most of them hated the Soviet regime of Marshal Stalin, especially such ethnic groups as the Georgians, and Tartars, and were not reluctant to fight against the Red Army. But they had no desire to fight the American and British armies.

Many of the German divisions were made up of rejects in poor physical shape. Men with flat feet, varicose veins, and stomach trouble could be depended on to defend a fixed position but not to move as rapidly as younger, healthier soldiers would. Many of von Rundstedt's divisions were badly under strength, some mere paper divisions, skeletons of what a fighting group should be.

As early as 1942, work had begun on strengthening the "Atlantic Wall," a line of fortifications behind which the German army would be invulnerable to any invasion. Foreign workers had been forced to build strongpoints, lay minefields, erect obstacles to landing craft and tanks, and unroll miles of barbed wire. This was to be the western bastion of "Fortress Europe" by which Hitler hoped to hold off the Allies until he had won in the East. The fortifications were heaviest along the French coast from the Pas de Calais to the Bay of Biscay; elsewhere they were sparse or nonexistent.

Von Rundstedt had nothing but contempt for the Atlantic Wall. He called it a propaganda trick, a showpiece, which could be pierced at any point by a determined attack. At best he hoped it would delay the Allies for twenty-four hours and allow him to bring up his panzer divisions for a crushing counterattack. This meant that he would have to guess where the Allies would land and have his tanks concentrated nearby to repel them.

To his anger, the field marshal found that he was not to control the critical tank divisions. Hitler did not trust Prussian officers who were not Nazis, and was determined that he alone would make the important decisions about strategy. He

sent his favorite soldier, Field Marshal Erwin Rommel, to inspect the Atlantic Wall and report on the work to him.

Rommel was fifty-three years old with a series of brilliant victories and one defeat behind him. In 1940 he had led his panzers in a stunning breakthrough in the Battle of France. Bypassing the Maginot Line, he had pushed boldly to the English Channel, cutting off the Anglo-French armies in Belgium and forcing their evacuation of the continent at Dunkirk. In Africa in 1942, he had pushed the British back steadily until his army was close to the vital Suez Canal. At the last minute, he had been defeated by Montgomery at El Alamein on November 1, 1942. Before his Afrika Korps had been destroyed, an ill Rommel had been recalled to Berlin by Hitler.

What he saw of the Atlantic Wall made Rommel furious. There semed to be no sense of urgency. Everywhere work was lagging. Only thousands of mines had been laid where there should have been millions. In his report, Rommel disagreed with von Rundstedt's strategy of waiting for the Allies to break through the wall and then counterattacking. From his own experience in the Egyptian desert, Rommel knew that an overwhelming Allied air superiority would make any daylight movement of tanks impossible. The panzers, he said, would have to be right behind the beaches. The Allies would have to be annihilated as they were struggling to land in France; otherwise the battle would be lost.

Impressed, Hitler made Rommel commander in chief of Army Group B. He would be responsible for defending the Channel coast from the German border to the Loire River,

*This German pillbox, shown
here after the Allied invasion,
was characteristic of the
fortifications that created
the "Atlantic Wall."*

including the Pas de Calais and Normandy. True, he would be under von Rundstedt but with direct access to Hitler. As for choosing between the two different strategies proposed, Hitler hesitated, finally leaving it to the two commanders to resolve. What the Fuehrer did do was to have a decisive effect on the battle: he ordered that two panzer divisions be put under his own control. They could not be moved without a direct order from Hitler himself.

This interference made von Rundstedt furious. It is hard to tell if he was more contemptuous of Hitler, whom he called "the Bohemian Corporal" or of Rommel, the "Kid Marshal." In any case, he had now lost control of more than half of the tanks he needed for a crushing counterattack. And he was saddled with a subordinate who disagreed with his strategy and could complain directly to Hitler.

Time and again, the Fuehrer interfered in the planning. He ordered that the Navy be responsible for the defense of all seaports and of all coastal artillery. The German Air Force, the Luftwaffe, controlled the airborne troops who were to be thrown into the battle as infantry. The Nazi S.S. divisions, troops recruited and trained by the Nazi party, were under the orders of Hitler's close friend, Heinrich Himmler. It was a hodgepodge of command, guaranteed to cause confusion. Von Rundstedt complained that the only decision he was allowed to make was changing the guard in front of his headquarters.

Hitler put his faith not in his commanders but in his own intuition. He had an almost mystic belief in his own genius in military matters. After all, he told himself, did I not defeat France in six weeks when my generals were all afraid to attack? The failure of the German army to defeat Russia he blamed on his generals for not following his orders. That these orders were ignored because they made no military sense never occurred to Hitler. His finger ranged over a map as he made frenzied guesses at the invasion beaches. Southern France, Holland, Normandy, Brittany, even Spain caught his eye and orders went out to strengthen the defenses of all of these places. His staff knew that most of these guesses were nonsense—Allied air cover could not reach them—but no one dared tell the vain Fuehrer the truth. All the German generals feared Hitler's hysterical tirades when he was shown the unpleasant truth.

In the last months before D-Day, Hitler's eye went more and more to Normandy. He knew that the Allies would have to capture a major port quickly, one that they could defend against counterattack. It could be Le Havre in the Pas de Calais, the shortest jump across the Channel, but what about Cherbourg? If the invaders cut the base of the Cotentin Peninsula, the port of Cherbourg at its northern tip would fall like a ripe apple. He ordered a crack parachute division sent to Normandy, right into the Cotentin.

Rommel took command of Army Group B and began a frantic buildup to strengthen the beach defenses. Tireless, he was constantly inspecting the work, never trusting anyone to get it done fast enough unless he was on the spot. He had fantastic plans for making all possible landing points a grave for any invader. Given enough time, he might have succeeded but time was running out. Spring had arrived and the invasion could not be far off.

Rommel dreamed of obstacles to invasion on a gigantic scale. First, the enemy landing craft would have their bottoms ripped open by steel stakes hidden underwater. Amphibious tanks would be blown up by minefields off the beaches or would get stuck on "hedgehogs" of triangular steel beams until the German guns finished them off. He even had the huge movable doors taken from the forts of the Maginot Line and buried offshore to slow the landings.

If the Allied troops did reach the beach, they would be met by more minefields, some 300 yards (273 m) deep. There would be concrete tank traps, miles of barbed wire, and other obstacles to get through. Meanwhile they would be under murderous fire from prepared positions just behind the beaches. Machine-gun and antitank guns would cut them down. Artillery in strongpoints would blast them along with mortars and rockets. From heavily protected concrete emplacements, big guns would take a terrible toll of men, landing craft, and the ships unloading just off the beaches. All these positions would support one another with overlapping fields of fire.

The Allied survivors who reached the sand dunes behind the beaches would be met by a different kind of fire. Pipes fed by kerosene tanks had been laid. At a touch of a button, the invaders would be burned to death.

To foil the Allied airborne soldiers, Rommel ordered the land behind the beaches to be flooded where possible. At what was to be Utah Beach, this left only five paths off the beach—the famous causeways that the Allied airborne had to capture. To injure the paratroopers as they floated down and smash gliders trying to land, Rommel had thousands of heavy tree trunks and telephone poles erected in all the likely fields. These were supposed to be connected by wires that would set off mines at the base of the poles if hit. Luckily for the Allies, there was not enough time to put in all the mines.

For three months, under Rommel's whip, the Germans and foreign slave laborers from all the Nazi-occupied countries worked to make the invasion a bloody repulse. Hitler and his generals knew what was at stake here: victory or defeat. If the invasion could be stopped, the Allies could not attempt it again for at least a year. In that time, the fifty divisions released from guarding the Atlantic Wall could be sent to the Eastern Front and drive back the advancing Soviet armies. There would be time to get into operation all the secret weapons of which the Fuehrer boasted, and win the war once and for all.

Hitler's intuition told him that the invasion would come at the beginning of May. When that passed and the Allies still did not appear, it seemed to Rommel he might have time to complete his work. Four million mines had been laid, but he wanted twenty million. More strongpoints, more heavy guns, more anti-airborne poles (now known as "Rommel's aspara-gus"). Every day he harassed his subordinates for these things and much more. It seemed he would never be satisfied until the Atlantic coast was one vast minefield with strong-points every ten yards (9 m).

The Germans kept an anxious eye on the weather. They knew as well as Eisenhower and his staff what conditions of tide, moon, clouds, and wind the invasion would need. Suit-able periods of good weather passed in May with no activity from the Allies. At the beginning of June, the first suitable time was from the 4th to the 8th. When the weathermen pre-dicted foul weather for this period, the Germans relaxed. Even Eisenhower would not be foolish enough to attempt an invasion in a storm. Besides, the German troops were exhausted by countless alerts. They could use a rest and so could Rommel. After months of tireless activity, he left France for a few days' leave at home. His generals were scheduled to attend a war-game exercise on June 6. One divi-sion was scheduled for maneuvers in the fields near the coast.

Even as Rommel and his generals departed, the Allied fleet was steaming across the Channel.

In England, the first week of June had been a time of anxiety, almost despair. D-Day had been set for dawn on June 5 and the immense movement of ships, men, and planes had to begin three days earlier so that they would arrive at the right time in front of the invasion beaches. Battleships and cruisers that would bombard enemy positions would be coming from Scotland and Northern Ireland, a long trip. Tens of thousands of men had to march from their holding camps down to the ships waiting in the southern ports. Other tens of thousands would have to move down and take their places in the camps, waiting for their turn to sail. The enormous numbers of tanks, trucks, jeeps, and other matériel had to be loaded in a certain order in thousands of ships and landing craft so they would be offloaded as needed on the beaches. It was a complicated operation on a scale that had never been attempted before. One hitch could spell disaster.

And it all depended on the weather.

At his advance headquarters overlooking Portsmouth harbor, Eisenhower, his chief lieutenants, and their staffs anxiously awaited the reports of a special team of weather forecasters. Twice a day, at 4 A.M. and 9 P.M. (all times are British Double Summer Time; German clocks were one hour earlier), these experts would brief them on the expected weather conditions for the next twenty-four hours. All through May, they had kept an eye on the weather brewing around Greenland, for it was from there that the weather over the invasion beaches would come a day later.

The first sign of trouble came with the formation of a low-pressure system far out at sea. This continued to build up and at the evening briefing on Saturday, June 3, the weathermen reported that there would be low clouds, high seas, strong winds, and poor visibility over Normandy from the 5th to the 7th—the days when the tides would be right. The invasion machinery was already in motion. Ships were sailing for the rendezvous points; others were being loaded with troops and would have to sail soon. If there was to be a delay, it would have to be announced soon or there would be no way to stop the invasion.

To postpone the landings was a serious decision. The armies were like a coiled spring waiting to be released. It would be a terrible blow to morale to leave the men cooped up aboard ships in the harbors. Would it be possible to keep the invasion secret when thousands now knew where they were to land?

Outside of headquarters, the skies were blue and the wind light. Eisenhower decided to wait until the next morning to see if the weather forecast did not improve. It was a slim chance but preferable to delaying the assault.

The slim chance failed. At 4:30 A.M. on Sunday, June 4, the weather team reported that it was now certain that conditions

*These soldiers—part of the invasion force—
receive instructions before moving into
position for the assault on Normandy.*

would be bad over the beaches. The weather would start to deteriorate that same night and would continue to be poor for three days. The greatest military enterprise in the history of warfare was at the mercy of clouds, winds, waves, and visibility.

Eisenhower asked for the opinions of his senior commanders. Montgomery wanted to go and damn the consequences. He was eager for battle and believed a delay would be worse than taking a chance. The Germans would never expect a landing in such foul weather, so surprise would be complete.

Admiral Ramsay was dubious. His smaller ships, he said, would have great difficulty sailing through the rough seas. Also, the low visibility meant that the bombardment by the big ships would be inaccurate. Leigh-Mallory was dead set against going ahead. He pointed out that low clouds and high winds would make the airborne landings a massacre. Paratroopers would be dragged by their chutes and gliders blown aside as they tried to land. Troop-carrier planes would be unable to find the right fields to drop their passengers.

Since the main flotilla would sail in just two hours, Eisenhower could not delay reaching a decision. Weighing all the factors, he ordered a postponement for twenty-four hours. D-Day was now June 6. H-Hour would remain at 6:30 A.M. All ships at sea were to be recalled and everyone prayed that the Germans had not spotted them in the Channel.

It was a very close thing. Most of the ships got the recall signal and turned back, but some minesweepers were perilously close to the Normandy coast before a British seaplane spotted them and flashed the signal. There was an unbelievable traffic jam as ships from distant ports had to take refuge in the crowded harbors on the south coast of England. The overwhelming Allied air superiority kept the Luftwaffe from flying over England during the day and spotting this activity.

By Sunday evening, the good weather had vanished in England as rain, low clouds, and gusty winds moved in. The forecasters had been right but that was no consolation to Eisenhower. He still had to decide if the invasion was to be put off until the next favorable tide period, two weeks away. If that had to be done, security, secrecy, and surprise would be almost impossible. His responsibility was horrendous. The fate of the Allied cause was in his hands. Others could advise but only the supreme commander could give the "go ahead" signal. Victory or defeat hung on his decision.

That night the weathermen repeated their forecast with one important difference. They had spotted a hole in the storm that meant that the weather would improve starting Monday night and continuing through Tuesday evening. It was only a guess but it was a chance for launching the invasion in this break in the storm.

Monday morning at the 4 A.M. briefing, the forecasters were more certain about the short period of improving weather. Now was the time for decision. Risk the success of Overlord on this slim chance or postpone for two weeks with its inevitable consequences. No man had carried such a heavy responsibility as Eisenhower did at this moment. Leigh-Mallory was still worried but thought it possible. Montgomery and Ramsay were in favor of going in.

"OK. Let's go," Eisenhower said. His voice was even and low pitched. There was no striving for dramatic effect. There was enough drama and chance for tragedy in the events that were now being unleashed.

The invasion of Normandy would begin at dawn the next morning.

In 1819, Lord Byron had written the following lines in the poem "Don Juan": " 'Twas on the sixth of June, about the hour of half past six . . . where the Fates change horses, making history change its tune." One hundred and twenty-five years before the event, Byron had picked D-Day and H-Hour.

Once the decision to go had been made, there was little for the senior commanders to do. All the plans had been

General Eisenhower talks to paratroopers of the
101st Airborne Division before they take off for France.

made, all the schedules set. A well-oiled machine had been put in motion and all the Supreme Commander could do was wait to find out if it was a success or a failure.

On the afternoon of June 5, Eisenhower issued a proclamation to his troops:

> Soldiers, Sailors and Airmen of the Allied Expeditionary Force: You are about to embark upon a Great Crusade . . . The eyes of the world are upon you . . . you will bring about the destruction of the German war machine, the elimination of Nazi tyranny over the oppressed peoples of Europe . . . Your task will not be an easy one. Your enemy is well trained, well equipped and battle-hardened. He will fight savagely . . . I have full confidence in your courage, devotion to duty and skill in battle. We will accept nothing less than full Victory. Good luck!

The Supreme Commander still worried about a possible tragedy in the airborne assault, as Leigh-Mallory had predicted. He went to one of the troop-carrier airfields where men of the 101st Airborne Division were getting ready. He walked among them, talking casually about home and country, examining the men's blackened faces, and the heavy equipment they carried. He grinned at the Mohawk scalplocks that some of the paratroopers wore and shared his confidence in the success of Overlord with the men who would soon be fighting in the fields of Normandy.

He did not tell the airborne troopers but in his pocket was a slip of paper with a few lines scribbled on it:

"Our landings in the Cherbourg-Havre area have failed . . . The troops, the air, and the navy did all that bravery and devotion to duty could do. If any blame or fault is attached to the attempt it is mine alone." As a soldier, Eisenhower knew how chancy a battle is. He had to be prepared for failure.

It stayed light in England at this time of year until almost 11 P.M. The paratroopers marched out to the waiting transport planes while the sun set. They were so heavily laden that some had to be pushed through the doorways and could not sit on the narrow bucket seats. Instead they knelt on the floor and rested their packs on the seat—as if in prayer.

A little after eleven, the planes taxied out to the end of the runway. It was dark now and all that could be seen was their wingtip lights and the bluish exhaust flames from the engines. A red flare curved up from the control tower. It was the signal to take off.

The lead plane gunned its engines, roared down the runway, and staggered into the air with its load of eighteen paratroopers. At over twenty airfields scattered over England, the same sight could be seen. The airborne was on its way to France. The aerial advance guard of the invasion was headed for battle.

CHAPTER IV

THE U.S. AIRBORNE ASSAULT

The first U.S. soldiers to land in Normandy floated down out of the dark skies at fifteen minutes past midnight on Tuesday, June 6, 1944. These were the "pathfinders," a specially trained group of airborne volunteers whose job it was to mark the drop zones for the two airborne divisions that would follow an hour later. They would set up marker lights, radio beacons, and radar transmitters so that the planes could find the right fields in the dark.

But first the pathfinders had to find the right fields. Speeding over the west coast of the Cotentin Peninsula at low altitude, the planes had run into heavy German antiaircraft fire, the dreaded "flak." This was the first time most of the pilots had been under fire and, understandably nervous about their unarmored transport planes being hit, they took evasive action. Turning rapidly from side to side, climbing and diving, made pinpoint navigation impossible. Less than a third of the 120 pathfinders had been dropped on the correct drop zone (DZ). The rest were scattered anywhere from one to three miles (1.6 to 4.8 km) away, a few even further. The lost men had great difficulty locating their positions in the dark and blundered about trying to find a landmark that was on their maps. Time was running out. Thirteen thousand paratroopers were already in the air and on their way to Norman-

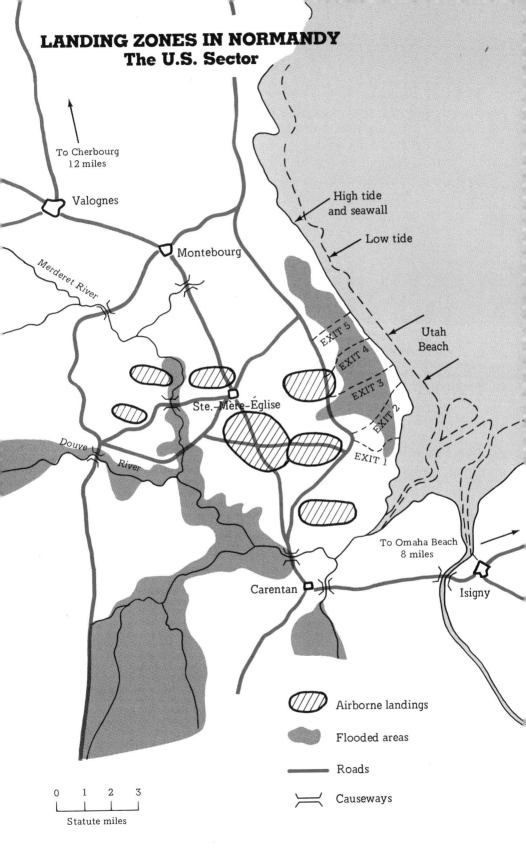

LANDING ZONES IN NORMANDY
The U.S. Sector

To Cherbourg
12 miles

Valognes

Montebourg

Merderet River

High tide
and seawall

Low tide

EXIT 5

EXIT 4

Utah
Beach

EXIT 3

Ste.-Mère-Église

EXIT 2

Douve

River

EXIT 1

To Omaha Beach
8 miles

Carentan

Isigny

Airborne landings

Flooded areas

Roads

Causeways

0   1   2   3

Statute miles

dy expecting to find their drop zones clearly marked by lights and radar signals.

At a dozen airfields in England, beginning about 11:30 P.M., the heavily laden paratroopers, crammed into over 800 twin-engine transport planes, had taken off for France. With only the blue formation lights on their wings showing, the formation crossed the south coast of England, flying low over the black waters of the Channel to avoid enemy radar. Halfway across the Channel, a ship was anchored that sent out a radio signal as a navigation "fix." This ship had been given the friendly name of "Hoboken."

Shortly after passing this point, the airborne armada turned left to avoid the guns on the German-held Channel Islands of Guernsey and Jersey. The sound of their engines had alerted the enemy and bright tracers and shells began to probe the night searching for them. No damage was done and soon the dark outline of the Cotentin coast could be seen dead ahead.

Major General Matthew B. Ridgway, commander of the 82nd Airborne Division, was standing near an open doorway watching the other planes in the formation. This is what he later said: "It was a beautiful clear night with a half-moon. We dropped down to jumping altitude when we crossed the coast and then—without warning—we went into a cloud bank and everything disappeared. You couldn't see a thing, not even the plane on your wing."

What the weathermen had not been able to predict was a thick cloud layer over the west coast of the Cotentin, right at the altitude at which the planes would cross. If the pathfinders had spotted it, they would not have been able to report it because of the strict radio silence that had been ordered. These clouds were to have a devastating effect on the airborne formation.

As soon as the planes plunged into the clouds, the formation broke apart and scattered. Some pilots, lacking any orders for this emergency situation, chose to climb above the cloud layer, some chose to dive and fly below it, and some

This photograph shows U.S. paratroopers
on a practice jump over England just
two weeks before D-Day.

flew straight through it on instruments. In an instant, all air discipline disappeared and it was every man for himself. Unable to see the lights of the man on his wing, each pilot had to make quick decisions to avoid collisions.

When they came out above, below, and through the clouds, most of the pilots found themselves alone. The rest of the formation had disappeared, leaving them to find the drop zone by themselves. At this moment, the German flak gunners opened fire.

Flying at low altitude and low airspeed, with no armor or self-sealing gas tanks, the C-47 troop-carrier planes were helpless. Bright tracers riddled them and shell explosions rocked them as they fought to control their aircraft and maintain the course to the DZs. Planes started to drop as they were hit. One C-47 exploded and crashed in flames near a small village. It began to look as if Leigh-Mallory had been right.

What saved them was their numbers—there were too many targets for the gunners—and the sheltering darkness. Although many of the planes suffered flak damage, only a few crashed, but most of them never found their assigned drop zones. On many of the fields there were no marker lights or radar signals to help them. The pathfinders in many cases were still struggling through the night, fighting off German patrols, and trying to locate the DZs.

With the dispersal caused by the cloud bank and the flak, it is surprising how many paratroopers were dropped on the correct DZ (or within a mile [1.6 km] of it). However, the majority jumped many miles from the correct spot, some into flooded areas not shown on aerial photographs.

Scattered over several hundred square miles of the Cotentin, disorganized, lost, separated from their units and their friends, the U.S. paratroopers now showed the individual initiative and courage of their kind. Like pioneers moving into hostile territory alone, they set out for the assigned assembly point with faith in themselves, their country, and their weapons. One man found another in the dark, the two then came upon a small group and joined up, soon there were a dozen or fifty or a hundred aggressive paratroopers moving through the night with one thought in mind: grab that bridge, seize that town, reach the causeway and hold it.

The wide dispersal of the airborne divisions had one favorable aspect. With hundreds of reports of paratroopers landing all over the peninsula, German headquarters were totally bewildered for hours. They hesitated to order an attack at any point until they knew where the main concentration of the U.S. airborne force would be. When they finally learned, it was too late.

At 2:11 A.M. (1:11 A.M. German time), an urgent telephone call interrupted the birthday party for General Erich Marcks, commander of the 84th Corps at St.-Lô. "Parachutists have landed east of the Orne!" reported a regimental commander in Caen to the startled Marcks. There was as yet no firm information as to how many or exactly where.

Marcks immediately called General Pemsel, chief of staff of the 7th Army, who quickly reached the correct answer to the mystery of the parachute landings. The invasion had begun. The 7th Army was ordered to the highest state of readiness, which meant that all beach positions were to be manned to repel landings from the sea, and the enemy paratroopers were to be attacked and destroyed. Twenty minutes later, Marcks telephoned Pemsel again and told him that paratroopers were being dropped at two places near Cherbourg. Fighting had already begun.

When these reports reached Rommel's headquarters, there was indecision and hesitation. Rommel himself was on leave in Germany, five.hundred miles (800 km) away, and his chief of staff was not convinced that this was the real invasion. The same was true at von Rundstedt's headquarters, where everyone was puzzled by reports of rubber dummies dressed as paratroopers being dropped over wide areas in Normandy, far from Cherbourg. When these dummy soldiers hit the ground, they set off a string of firecrackers as if firing guns. The Germans had convinced themselves that the main attack had to come in the Pas de Calais, so the airborne attack in Normandy was at best a feint, trying to draw the German armies away from Calais.

The confusion in the minds of the German planners was understandable. The reports that came flooding in were often not only inaccurate but contradictory. How could anyone explain the wide scattering of the paratroopers, the rubber dummies, the absence of any landing from the sea without which the paratroopers were doomed? Then, too, the weather was foul, much too bad for the invasion (the Germans did not know that the weather was clearing). Even Eisenhower, they said, would not risk failure by trying to land in this weather.

While they hesitated, the intelligence staff came up with an inspired explanation: what had been reported as paratroopers were really bomber crews jumping from their stricken planes or possibly agents being parachuted to join the French resistance.

Three hours after the first pathfinders had dropped into Normandy, only the 7th Army staff was convinced that the invasion had begun. At higher headquarters, the attitude was "wait and see." After all, the whole affair could turn out to be insignificant—a raid or a minor diversion. Rommel's chief of staff gave his opinion that "for the time being, this is not to be considered a major operation."

To add to the uncertainty and confusion, many senior German generals, like Rommel, were away from their posts. Most of them had already left for the war games exercise at Rennes. The problem they were to study was an airborne and seaborne invasion of Normandy!

And while the Germans waited, two U.S. airborne divisions parachuted and glided into the Cotentin and one British airborne division landed east of the Orne. Almost twenty-five thousand Allied parachutists and glider troops were even then fighting to gain their objectives.

And out at sea, the five thousand ships of the Allied invasion fleet were anchored twelve miles (19 km) from the invasion beaches. At first light, they would begin the bombardment and then land their troops.

While the German generals debated and hesitated, a deadly game of hide-and-seek was going on among the hedgerows of the Cotentin Peninsula. Thirteen thousand paratroopers, widely scattered by the cloud bank and the intense antiaircraft fire, were creeping through the dark night trying to find out where they had been dropped and where the rest of their units were. The German troops in the Cotentin could not locate all the widely scattered *Fallschirmjäger* (paratroopers). The telephone lines between German units had been cut by the U.S. airborne soldiers and the German radios jammed by Allied interference. They did not know how many of the enemy had landed or what their objectives were. Nervous and trigger-happy, small groups of U.S. and German soldiers groped through the dark, trying to find friends and avoid foes.

For the Americans of the two airborne divisions, it was a frustrating experience. Except for one regiment of the 101st that landed together, most could not find the landmarks they had expected. Also, the Germans had flooded the area around the Douve and Merderet rivers, so that what had appeared to be firm ground on aerial photographs turned out to be marshland. Dragged down by their heavy packs or caught in the parachute shrouds, paratroopers drowned in three feet (.9 m) of water. Vital equipment canisters were dropped into these marshes and sank. Only forty percent of this equipment was found and recovered.

In the blackness, life or death depended on an instant and correct answer to a whispered challenge. Men of the 101st had been given toy "clickers" for identification and the fields of Normandy were filled with soft click-clicks as men tried to find their buddies. Men died in short, violent encounters, often without seeing one another. Any noise, any late answer to a challenge, any shadow brought a burst of fire. The cows and horses of Normandy suffered large losses from frightened, trigger-happy soldiers.

One tragic incident occurred in Sainte-Mère-Église, an important crossroads town that was to be captured by the 82nd Airborne. Shortly after one o'clock in the morning, the townspeople were awakened by the cry of "Fire!" A flare from a bomber had set the roof of a villa facing the town square afire. Firemen and a volunteer bucket brigade began to fight the blaze, watched by the German garrison and nearby antiaircraft crews.

Suddenly, there was a dull, low growling in the distance. It grew to a roar and hundreds of planes flew low over the town, illuminated by the light from the fire. Soon countless parachutes could be seen as the amazed Germans shouted "*Fallschirmjäger!*" and ran for their guns. The burning house was forgotten as the French fled to their homes and the Germans fired at the planes and parachutists.

Between the town and the Merderet River, the planes dropped a paratroop regiment accurately—one of the best drops of the night. But some of the planes dropped their "sticks" (all the paratroopers in one plane are called a "stick") too early and they came down right on the town. Swinging helplessly in their parachute harnesses, the paratroopers were easy targets for the alerted German garrison. They were shot down as they tumbled into the square, dangled from trees, or floated overhead. One parachutist was left dangling on the side of the church when his chute snagged the steeple. He played dead but was later captured, deafened by the tolling of the church bell. One man floated into the burning villa and disappeared amid the explosions of the ammunition he was carrying.

When paratroopers of the 101st arrived at Sainte-Mère-Église an hour later, they found the bodies of their comrades still lying in the square or hanging from their parachute shrouds. The town was to be the first to be liberated, but at a terrible cost.

Generals among the paratroopers were not exempt from being lost in the confusion that night. The commander of the 101st, Major General Maxwell Taylor, came down in a field without a man in sight. He wandered for thirty minutes before he found another soldier, a private. Like long-lost brothers, they hugged each other, each happy to see a friendly face. It would be twelve hours before there were enough men for General Taylor to even think of carrying out his orders.)

The assistant commander of the 82nd, thirty-six-year-old Brigadier General James Gavin, also landed alone and spent some time finding the other twenty men of his stick. They had landed right on the edge of the flooded Merderet and were soon joined by men who crawled out of the marsh. All of their heavy equipment had been lost. There was not one antitank gun to challenge the German armor they could hear moving around them. With 150 riflemen, Gavin headed for the bridge over the Merderet that was one of his unit's objectives. He arrived too late. German tanks held the other end of the bridge and there was no way to fight them. The bridge was only taken four days later when tanks arrived from Utah Beach.

It was a frantic, nervous night of ambush and skirmish. The hedgerows divided the battle area into small field-sized arenas. One could not see into the next field without peering over the top, and that could be fatal. Here a hedgerow was not a thin line of small shrubs. The French *bocage* was an earth-packed mound four to six feet (1.2 to 1.8 m) high, filled with the thick roots of the tall poplars that grew out of them. They were natural breastworks and an enemy could be on the other side of a hedgerow and still be invisible. Some of the most brutal and frustrating fighting of the war would be in this *bocage* country.

The Americans showed wonderful initiative, a willingness to take any risk regardless of how few soldiers were available to get the job done. With only a dozen men, a colonel attacked a powerful battery that threatened Utah. Luckily, he found it deserted, the crews driven off by Allied air raids. Another colonel rounded up two hundred of his men and destroyed two bridges over the Douve River to keep German panzers out of the Cotentin. Although only at half strength, one regiment of the 101st attacked the strong German positions covering the land sides of two causeways to Utah Beach. After a sharp fight, the Germans were driven off and the seaborne assault would be able to get inland.

Just before dawn, the two airborne divisions were reinforced by over a hundred Waco gliders bringing in the crucial antitank guns. The planes towing these big motorless craft came through the same clouds and the same intense antiaircraft fire as the paratroopers. Landing the gliders in the dark with only a single signal lamp to guide them was a difficult task and the glider pilots and their passengers paid the price for their inexperience. The anti-glider poles, the hedgerows that were like stone walls, the flooded areas, the antiaircraft fire—all these took a high toll. The gliders released from the 300-foot (91-m) nylon towropes and came down with a sighing sound. It had to be done. The antitank guns were badly needed.

The first glider to land in the 101st area slid over the wet grass and smashed into the trees. In the wreckage was the body of the division's second-in-command, Brigadier General Don Pratt. He had been sitting in the jeep the glider carried, next to his aide who was unhurt. Pratt was the first U.S. general to be killed in the invasion.

The Germans, too, lost a general that night. Major General Wilhelm Falley had been en route to Rennes for the war games when all the Allied planes in the vicinity made him decide to return to his post. As he sped down a dark road, paratroopers ambushed his car and he died in a hail of machine-gun bullets.

All through the night, the U.S. paratroopers fought to throw the enemy off balance. As more and more men found their units, the airborne strength grew. Most objectives were finally taken, mainly by small groups of determined fighters.

The airborne could be reinforced by sea or air, but the German losses could not be replaced. The Cotentin had been effectively sealed off even with the wide scattering of the invading divisions. Unless there was a strong counterattack—and that meant tanks—the U.S. airborne would win the battle.

And on the left flank (as seen from the sea), the British airborne was already in action.

CHAPTER

THE
BRITISH
AIRBORNE
ASSAULT

At almost the exact moment that the U.S. pathfinders leaped from their planes, sixty miles (96 km) to the east, the British pathfinders were also jumping into the night sky. No one will ever know who was the first Allied soldier to land on French soil during Overlord, but he was without doubt either a U.S. or British pathfinder.

The job of the British 6th Airborne Division was to protect the British invasion beaches from an attack by the German panzers located east of Caen (see map, page 61). In addition, they had to capture and destroy a heavily defended battery of big guns at Merville that could cause serious damage to Sword, the easternmost of the British beaches. Unless the battery was knocked out before dawn, bombers and naval gunfire would try to do the job, but the concrete fort in which the German guns were located was built to withstand this type of bombardment. The only hope was for the paratroopers to get inside, through minefields and barbed wire, and blow it up.

The plan called for the pathfinders to drop shortly after midnight and mark the fields for the main parachute force arriving thirty minutes later. At the same time, six big Horsa gliders would crash-land on the two bridges crossing the Orne River and nearby Caen Canal. These bridges were to be seized intact since they were necessary for reinforcements from the beaches to reach the airborne. Since it was known that the Germans would blow up the bridges at the first sign of an attack, the only way to grab them intact was a *coup de main*, a lightning attack by a small force.

The main parachute force would drop between the two bridges and the Dives River, five miles (8 km) to the east. Their job was to destroy the five bridges across the Dives and attack the Merville battery. The Germans had flooded the valley of the Dives for a width of about a mile (1.6 km). With the bridges gone, the panzers would not be able to attack the invasion beaches from the east. If they came in from the south, between the Orne and the Dives, they would be met by British antitank guns brought in by gliders.

It was a bold and daring plan that depended on split-second timing, ruthless determination to succeed at all costs, and a great deal of luck.

The planes carrying the pathfinders made the first mistake. Errors in navigation and an unexpected wind meant that the pathfinders dropped too far east of the real landing zones. With the main parachute force coming in in half an hour, there was not time to march back, so the pathfinders set up their marker lights and radio beacons in suitable fields near the point where they had been dropped. Unfortunately, it was dangerously close to a large forest called the Bois de Bavent, and to the flooded valley of the Dives River.

Even as the pathfinders were jumping from their planes, six Horsa gliders carrying 160 soldiers of a crack airborne regiment were releasing their towropes over the French coast. This was the specially trained *coup de main* force that was attacking the bridges over the Orne River and the Caen Canal. They were commanded by Major John Howard, a thirty-year-old company commander, flying his first airborne mission.

The gliders had cut loose from the Halifax bombers that towed them at an altitude of over five thousand feet (1,524 m), just as they reached the French coast. The bridges were eight miles (13 km) away, but from this height the gliders

British glider pilots composed a message
for Hitler as they prepared for their
part in the D-Day invasion.

could swoop down silently and crash-land close enough to the bridges so that the Germans would not have time to blow them up. It would have to be a crash landing, for there were no suitable fields close to the bridges and aerial photos had shown that the Germans were erecting large poles in all the fields to impale any gliders.

Once off the towropes, the noise of the slipstream died to a soft whisper, and silently the six Horsas slid down through scattered clouds, following the clear moonlit paths of the river and the canal. It was just like the training film the British glider pilots had been shown, made with a model of the terrain. The river, the canal, the roads, even the farms had been exactly right.

Seven minutes after crossing the coast, they sighted their targets: the two bridges. Lowering their huge flaps for a steep dive, the Horsas plunged down for the final approach. Inside the gliders, the soldiers linked arms, braced themselves for the impact, and lifted their feet in case the poles ripped out the wooden floor (the Horsa glider was made of plywood).

Three gliders headed for the canal bridge and the other three for the Orne bridge, about a quarter-mile (0.4 km) away. The lead Horsa, carrying Major Howard, touched down at seventy-five miles an hour (120 kph) and careered across the small field toward the canal bridge. With a thunderous roar, it plowed through the ground on its belly, leaving its landing gear behind. The plywood fuselage cracked and ripped, throwing large pieces of wood in all directions. Finally it shuddered to a stop, not twenty yards (18 m) from the bridge.

Inside, the stunned soldiers reacted as if by instinct, as well-trained men do. The doorway of the glider had collapsed under the impact, but there was a big gaping hole in the fuselage, through which they leaped and ran toward the bridge.

The German sentry stared open-mouthed at the men with blackened faces who were running toward him, then ran.

The small German garrison was taken completely by surprise. There was time to fire only one burst from a machine gun, killing a lieutenant; then the wave of British glider troops smashed into their trenches and the Germans fled. Within three minutes, the Caen Canal bridge was taken.

Quickly, the demolition wires strung along the bridge were cut. To their surprise, the British found that the explosive charges had not been put in place. They were later found neatly stacked at the far end of the bridge.

Taking the Orne bridge, too, had been amazingly easy. That was lucky because only two gliders landed close enough to attack—and one of those was a quarter of a mile (0.4 km) away. The third glider had released at the wrong point and ended up on the other side of the Dives River. The British troops nearest the bridge did not wait for the others, however. They attacked immediately, and the German defenders broke and ran. By the time the troops from the second glider walked the quarter-mile, the bridge was taken.

Meanwhile Major Howard was trying to raise brigade headquarters on his radio to report his successful capture of the two bridges intact. The code signal for taking the canal bridge was "ham." For capturing the Orne bridge, it was "jam." Howard listened impatiently as his radio operator repeated "ham and jam, ham and jam." There was no reply. Exasperated, the radio man shouted, "ham and bloody jam!" This triumphal signal was never received. The brigade's radios had been lost in the parachute drop. This was the first indication that something had gone terribly wrong for the British paratroopers. In fact, after a brilliant beginning, the whole British airborne assault was a near disaster.

It was the same story as in the U.S. airborne sector in the Cotentin: poor aerial navigation, clouds, unpredicted winds, and evasive maneuvering by pilots facing flak for the first time. First, the pathfinders had been dropped in the wrong place so that now their marker lights and radio beacons were too far east. Navigators mistook the flooded Dives River for

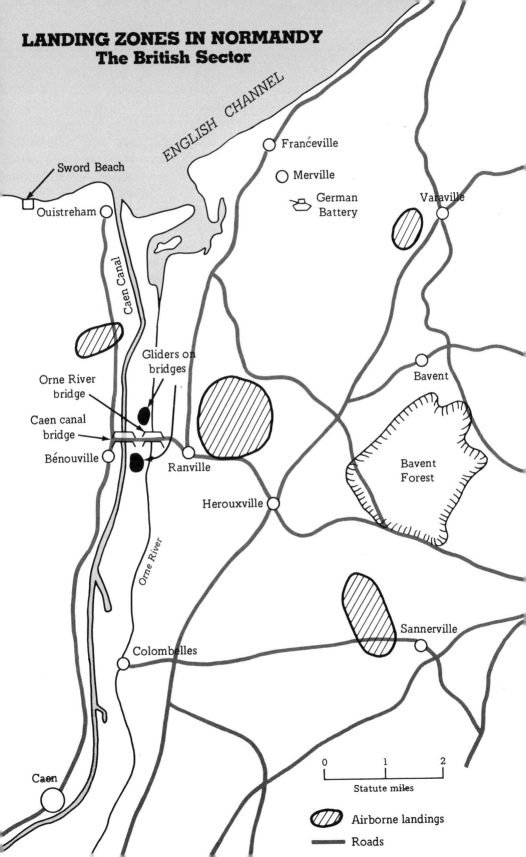

LANDING ZONES IN NORMANDY
The British Sector

ENGLISH CHANNEL

Franceville

Merville

German Battery

Varaville

Sword Beach

Ouistreham

Caen Canal

Gliders on bridges

Bavent

Orne River bridge

Caen canal bridge

Bénouville

Ranville

Bavent Forest

Herouxville

Orne River

Sannerville

Colombelles

Caen

0   1   2

Statute miles

Airborne landings

Roads

the Orne, so paratroopers were dropped east of the Dives, far from the landing zones where they were expected. Violently swinging planes trying to escape shells knocked their passengers off their feet as they struggled to reach the doors, which delayed the jumps. All this combined to scatter the parachutists of the 6th Airborne Division over a hundred square miles (160 sq km). Many were dropped into the flooded marshes of the Dives and disappeared forever. It was a fiasco.

The commander of the attack on the Merville battery was Lieutenant Colonel T. B. H. Otway. As he was swinging down in his parachute, he was horrified to see that he was heading directly for a German battalion headquarters. No pulling on the shroud lines prevented him from hitting the building and dropping into a garden. There were two other troopers already there and as the sleepy Germans opened a window to see what the noise was, a private threw a brick through the window. Thinking it was a grenade, the Germans ducked, allowing Otway and his men to escape.

When he finally arrived late at the rendezvous, Otway found only 150 of the 750 men who had jumped with him. Worse, all their heavy equipment needed for the attack was gone: no mortars, no antitank guns, no mine detectors, no signal equipment. There was only one heavy machine gun and no sign of the engineers who were to blow up the enemy guns.

There were agonizing decisions for the twenty-nine-year-old commanding officer to make. His plan had called for a reconnaissance platoon to advance early, cut the outer wire, and find a path through the first minefield. There was no news of them. Where were they? Also, three Horsa gliders carrying sixty men were supposed to crash-land right on the guns when Otway's men began their attack. The gliders would go in only if they received a signal from the ground that all was ready; otherwise it would be suicide for them. But the marker lights to give this "go ahead" signal had been lost. All in all, it looked like the attack on the Merville battery was doomed to failure and that the German guns would wreak havoc on the British beaches and the ships offloading there.

Otway waited as long as he could, hoping more of his men would find the rendezvous, then gave the order to move out. It was still almost two miles (3.2 km) to the battery and the Germans were alerted. Just before three o'clock, the British paratroopers slipped into the woods and began their march. With only one-fifth of the mission available, they would still try to capture the guns.

In absolute silence, they made their way through the woods. Overhead they heard the sound of plane engines as the main glider force headed for its landing zones. A German antiaircraft battery was firing on it and Otway's men were tempted to attack the guns, but they were late already and firing would give away their position. In single file they continued their advance.

The commander of the reconnaissance party found Otway at the head of the file. He reported that the first wire had been cut and a path found through the first minefield. It had been a grim job, done by hand, for the mine detectors had been lost in the drop, along with the white tape to mark the clear path. Now the safe road was marked by two furrows dug in the earth with the troopers' heels.

The bad news was that the bomber attack had been a failure. Not one bomb had hit the battery position. Instead the RAF had dropped their bombs on the landing fields of the reconnaissance party. There can be nothing more frightening than parachuting down on a field being blown up by heavy bombs.

By 4:30 A.M. Otway's men were in position on the edge of the Merville battery. Any second now the gliders would come in and there was still no way to signal them to attack. Without that signal the gliders would land anywhere they could, except on the concrete emplacement that held the guns.

Two gliders and their towplanes arrived on time (the

third had broken its towrope over England). Otway watched in anguish as the Horsas cast off, circled looking for the signal, then disappeared from sight as they came down in fields far from the battery. Now there was nothing to be done but attack the two hundred German defenders dug in behind barbed wire and wide minefields. Otway gave the order and his yelling men threw themselves into a storm of mortar and machine-gun fire. They made straight for the guns, firing on the Germans outside the concrete fort only to make them keep their heads down. Here and there men fell. The whole scene was lit by the bright tracers and the explosions of mortar shells. It was like a ghastly play straight out of hell.

In twenty minutes it was over. The paratroopers had quickly reached the guns, disregarding terrible losses, and had wiped out the defenders inside by firing through the gun ports. In the trenches outside, the surviving Germans, only twenty-two in all, surrendered to the dreaded "Red Devils," as they called the British paratroopers. The Merville guns (which turned out to be only 75-mm [3-inch] cannon instead of the reported 150s [6-inch]) were blown up by stuffing German bombs in their breeches.

By reckless determination and brutal hand-to-hand fighting, Otway's command had won—but at a price. Of the hundred fifty men who had started the charge, half were dead or wounded. The signal for success was sent off to the fleet just fifteen minutes before the ships would have started their bombardment of the battery. It had been a very close thing.

At 3:30, the commanding general of the 6th Airborne Division arrived with the main glider force. As he surveyed the landing field and listened to the reports, there was enough reason for Major General Richard Gale to be alarmed. Although the paratroopers had cleared the meadows in time, fifty of the seventy-two Horsas that had left England all seemed intent on landing in the same field. They came in too fast, tearing off landing gear, wings, tails, burying their noses in the soft

Horsa gliders lie broken in a field in Normandy.

ground and turning over. All too often, a landing glider would hit one already on the ground, and pieces of plywood were flying everywhere. Men leaving one glider or unloading the cargo were in danger of being killed by a Horsa out of control. It was hard to believe that anyone or anything could survive.

General Gale refused to be upset. Over six feet (1.8 m) tall, stocky, with a reddish face and a fierce-looking mustache, he was a thirty-year veteran of the Army and an experienced airborne commander. He had seen this foul-up on night glider landings before and he knew that few men would be hurt and that most of the jeeps and antitank guns would be in working order. When news began to trickle in of the wide dispersal of the paratroopers, particularly Otway's command, he still was not upset. He had faith in his men, the men he had trained to act on their own initiative even when alone behind enemy lines. Gale knew that the job would get done.

And it was done brilliantly under the most difficult conditions. By dawn, the Merville battery had been destroyed and the five bridges over the Dives River had been blown up. As Gale knew, it was small, isolated groups—separated from the larger force that had been assigned to destroy a given bridge—that finally did the job. In one case it was a single sergeant who, finding himself alone after the drop, marched to the nearest bridge, borrowed explosives from some lost soldiers, and blew the center span of the bridge into the river. Often the "Red Devils" had to fight their way through German lines to reach their objectives. One by one, the bridges were destroyed and the threat of German tanks hitting the invasion beaches from the east vanished. The antitank guns that Gale's men were rescuing from the smashed Horsas were enough to block any panzer attack from the south.

Despite the errors and mistakes by the air force (including the bombing of Otway's men by Allied planes), the British 6th Airborne Division had succeeded in carrying out every one of its missions. The left flank of the invasion was secure.

CHAPTER VI

THE U.S. BEACHES

The ships of the Utah Beach assault force dropped anchor at 2:30 A.M. It was still four hours before the landings would begin but there was a lot of work to be done. Minesweepers were busy clearing out the area and patrol craft were taking up positions on the flanks to guide the landing craft to the beach.

Broken clouds filled the threatening sky and a twenty-mile-an-hour wind blew from the land. The sea was choppy with waves three to six feet (.9 to 1.8 m) high slapping against the sides of the 865 ships in the fleet. The sun would rise a few minutes before 6 A.M. and as soon as the visibility allowed, the first bombardment would begin. In the darkness, the big ships with the big guns slipped closer to the shore and anchored. There were battleships, cruisers, destroyers, monitors, and rocket craft, all waiting to pour a storm of steel on the enemy defenses.

Shortly after 4 A.M., rope ladders were dropped over the sides of the troop transports, landing craft were lowered into the water, and loading began. Heavily laden, the men of the first assault wave (4th Infantry Division) carefully lowered themselves down the wet, slippery ladders and jumped into the LCIs (landing craft, infantry) banging against the sides of their transport. There were remarkably few accidents, few broken bones or smashed teeth, despite the choppy sea, the slick ropes, and the darkness. It was all done in almost complete silence, with only a few whispered commands and curses.

While the men were loading, LCTs (landing craft, tanks) were being lifted out of their mother ships and put into the water. Each LCT carried four amphibious Sherman tanks—each of which had a small propeller in the rear and a large inflatable canvas life belt. These tanks would be taken to within three miles (4.8 km) of the beach, then would "swim" the rest of the way. They would be needed to help the infantry overcome the German trenches and machine-gun nests.

After the LCIs were filled and the LCTs lowered into the water, they began to circle behind the fleet, waiting for the order to move toward the beach. Engineers would go in first, to remove obstacles and blow holes in the low concrete seawall at the base of the dunes. This was necessary if the tanks were to get through to support the infantry.

Waiting is always the hardest part of any combat operation. To the men jammed into the steel landing craft, wet from the spray that broke over the bow, seasick from the violent motions as the craft wallowed in the waves, the wait seemed interminable. In their imaginations, they had already dreamed up all the terrors of landing in the face of enemy fire. Now anything was better than being soaked and seasick.

Since it would take them ninety minutes to reach the beach, the landing craft started just before 5 A.M. As they sped toward the still-invisible shore, the soldiers heard the sound of heavy naval guns in the distance. Allied warships were firing on German batteries that had been harassing the minesweepers and patrol craft.

At 5:40 A.M., the naval bombardment began. With ear-splitting crashes, the big guns hurled a rain of steel on the enemy defenses. From six miles (9.7 km) out, the battleships and cruisers fired on assigned targets. Closer in, destroyers and rocket ships added to the terrible destruction. When the sun came up, the men in the landing craft could see nothing of Utah Beach but a cloud of dirty smoke and dust, in the midst of which were sprinkled the bright flames of exploding shells. Allied planes bombed German strongpoints, corrected the fire of the Allied ships, and laid a smoke screen between the landing craft and the shore.

Everything went according to plan except for one miscalculation that proved to be a stroke of luck. Because the beach was hidden beneath the smoke and dust, the navy crewmen of the landing craft could not see anything to guide on. Unaware of a swift current near the shore, they failed to correct for the drift and finally put their ships in shallow water about a mile (1.6 km) south of the designated beach. Fortunately, the German defenses were weak at this point, while the original landing spot was covered by two enemy batteries that would have taken a heavy toll of the landing troops. Also, the new beach was protected from the choppy waters by a spit of land and the U.S. soldiers were able to wade the last hundred yards (91 m) with almost no losses from either drownings or enemy fire. The LCTs were able to launch their tanks in a fairly calm sea one mile (1.6 km) out instead of in dangerous choppy waters three miles (4.8 km) out. Supported by the tanks, the first assault wave rushed across the beach, moved through the holes in the seawall that the engineers had made, and drove the few German defenders from their trenches.

Their progress was so rapid that it was decided by Brigadier General Theodore Roosevelt, Jr., who had waded ashore with the first wave—armed only with a cane and a pistol—that all follow-up troops would land at the same spot. President Teddy Roosevelt's oldest son, the general made a vital decision that avoided confusion and great losses. He continued in command until his superior landed. Six days later, he would die of a heart attack at fifty-seven.

The new beach was not taken bloodlessly. The U.S. destroyer *Corry* hit a mine, broke in two, and sank, with many dead. An LCT also struck a floating mine and went down with its crew and four amphibious tanks. German bat-

*These men were among the first assault troops
to go ashore at Utah Beach on D-Day.*

teries began to fire on the beach despite the dense screen of dust and smoke, and men died from this blind shooting. But the first wave swept up over the dunes to the causeways through the flooded area, and reinforcements poured in almost unopposed—tanks, trucks, antitank guns, tons of supplies. By 8 A.M., the beachhead was secured at the cost of less than two hundred casualties.

The German regiment defending the beach fought without enthusiasm, then, faced with being overrun, surrendered. Among the prisoners were many anti-Soviet Russians who had agreed to serve in the Wehrmacht rather than starve in prisoner-of-war camps. They had absolutely no interest in dying for Hitler's Germany and gave up at the first opportunity.

Shortly after 11 A.M., Captain George Mabry of the U.S. 4th Infantry Division stood at the beach end of the first causeway and waved an orange flag. This was the agreed-on signal for identifying the assault troops to the airborne. At the far end of the causeway, paratroopers of the 101st Airborne popped up and waved back. Mabry reported to General Maxwell Taylor, commander of the 101st, and learned that three of the causeways had been secured. The road off the beach was open and the advance inland began.

By luck, an unknown current, and the courage of the LCT control officer who brought the tanks close to the beach, the landings at Utah had been an overwhelming success.

At Omaha, the second U.S. beach, twelve miles (19 km) to the east, it was a very different story. There all the luck was bad.

At first it seemed that all would go well. In the darkness, the men of the first wave, fifteen hundred soldiers of the U.S. 29th and 1st Infantry divisions, climbed down the ladders into the wallowing landing craft. Sixteen LCTs were lowered by cranes from their mother ships and began to circle, waiting for the signal to go in. There were dozens of DUKWs, amphibious vehicles affectionately called "ducks," that could swim and drive up on the beach carrying 105mm (4-inch) cannon. With the swimming tanks, they should be able to handle any pillbox or concrete bunker.

Promptly at ten minutes to six, the naval bombardment began. Shells of all calibers pounded the German positions on top of the high bluffs that looked down on Omaha. For thirty-five minutes, the known enemy gun emplacements were hit time and again. It seemed that nothing could survive the rain of high explosives that swept the hills and the fields behind it where the enemy trenches were dug. In addition, almost five hundred heavy bombers dropped over a thousand tons (900 mt) of bombs despite the poor visibility that made accuracy difficult.

Allied intelligence had reported that Omaha Beach was defended by two German divisions; one made up of young veterans, was first-class, the other third-rate. At any time, two regiments (about 2,000 men) would be manning the beach defenses, with four other regiments in reserve several miles away at Bayeux. Three lines of underwater obstacles made of steel and concrete would be exposed at low tide. Then there would be two hundred yards (182 m) of hard sand to the first shelter, a low cobblestone seawall near the base of the bluffs. There were five gullies leading up to the top of the bluffs, all mined and covered by machine guns. Hundreds of barbed-wire fences protected the approaches to the guns mounted in the concrete emplacements at the top. Of particular concern were the six heavy cannon on top of the Pointe du Hoc, which could take a heavy toll of the fleet, the landing craft, and the troops on the beach as they struggled out of the water. Two specially trained Ranger battalions had been ordered to capture these guns by climbing the 150-foot-high (46-m) cliff. The Rangers were an elite group of volunteers, commandos trained to do the tough jobs.

No one had expected it to be a walkover, but everyone was confident that the naval and air bombardment would knock out any serious opposition. But intelligence had failed to spot many of the well-camouflaged gun positions or to realize that fifteen- and twenty-foot-thick (4.6- and 6.1-m) walls made them safe from even the biggest shells. The Germans on top of the bluffs looked right down on the whole length of Omaha Beach and could sweep every inch of it with murderous rifle, machine-gun, mortar, and artillery fire. Neither the naval nor the air bombardment was the least bit effective in knocking out the extensive enemy defenses. The Germans waited for the shelling and bombing to stop and for the landing craft to come into range of their guns.

Meanwhile, out at sea, the invasion fleet was already in serious trouble. Three German torpedo boats roared out of the smoke screen that had been laid down to protect the Allied fleet, fired eighteen torpedoes, and disappeared. Hit dead center, the Norwegian destroyer *Svenner* broke in two and sank within minutes. This was the only enemy naval attack on D-Day but the fear of more torpdedo attacks kept the fleet jumpy.

Just like the troops approaching Utah, the men in the landing craft were wet, cold, nervous, and most were seasick. They were still far enough from the beach so that no enemy guns had fired on them, but already they would have faced anything rather than the nausea and vomiting. The roar of the diesel engines deafened them and they had to shout to make themselves heard by the man next to them. It was a miserable trip and they were still unaware of what lay ahead.

The first indication that things were going wrong came when the amphibious tanks rolled out of the LCTs about three miles (4.8 km) from land. As the ramps dropped and the tanks drove into the choppy waters, the sea tore open the inflated canvas life belts and slopped into the engine compartments. With all buoyancy lost, the first twenty-seven tanks disappeared beneath the waves. Hatches opened and some of the crews escaped, but many were carried down to the Channel floor. In the same way, dozens of the "ducks" foundered and sank, with the loss of the precious heavy cannon.

Seeing the tanks sink, the remaining LCTs continued on to within a mile (1.6 km) of the beach before sending their tanks into the water. Only half the tanks and a few of the 105mm (4-inch) guns reached Omaha. The loss of the others cost many lives.

Relentlessly the swarm of landing craft moved toward the beach. Water poured over the sides and the men bailed desperately to keep the boats from sinking. Ten LCIs foundered and sank, leaving their passengers struggling in the sea. Heavily laden, some of the men disappeared beneath the waves without a cry. Others yelled for help from the passing craft, but the orders had been strict: no stopping for survivors. That was a job for other boats coming behind them.

Now they could see the beach—or rather the smoke, dust, and red flashes that marked Omaha. Heavy shells still roared overhead and smashed into the bluffs. Rockets wooshed past and exploded on the sands. The men huddled behind the steel bow ramps of the LCIs, prayed and waited. There was still no fire from the enemy and that worried them. The veterans of the 1st Division—the "Big Red One"—could not believe that all resistance had been wiped out. They had fought the Germans in North Africa and knew them to be tough fighters. The men of the 29th Division were going into their first battle and it would be at what would later be called "Bloody Omaha."

An LCT dropped its ramp in calmer water close to the beach—and hit a mine. It vanished in a tremendous explosion out of which a thirty-ton (27-mt) tank was thrown high into the air. There would be four fewer tanks to crawl up on the sand and cover the assault troops.

At 6:25 A.M., five minutes before the assault troops reached the beach, the naval bombardment had shifted to targets inland to prevent any reinforcements from reaching the enemy troops closer to the landing forces. Largely untouched by the shelling and bombs, the Germans ran to their guns and waited for the long line of LCIs to come within range. From their positions on top of the bluffs, they had a clear field of fire on every part of the five-mile-long (8-km) beach.

The thirty surviving amphibious tanks came in first. They waddled up to the steel-and-concrete obstacles, exposed in the low tide, and at once came under fire from German artillery. Ten tanks were knocked out in the first few minutes, some burning fiercely as the crews tried to escape under machine-gun fire. Without the protection of the tanks, the engineers struggling to blow paths through the hedgerows and barbed wire were easy targets. Many of the obstacles were mined and enemy snipers aimed at the mines as the engineers worked frantically to defuse them, setting off huge explosions. There were unmarked minefields, new types of obstacles, and booby traps. Soon half the engineers were casualties, many blown up by their own explosives. Only a few paths had been cleared through the obstacles and minefields.

Then the uneven line of landing craft carrying the first assault wave of infantry reached the beach. For the last four hundred yards (364 m), they had been under fire, intense, accurate, and withering. Two LCIs had been sunk by shellfire and the surviving soldiers had leaped into the water. Some managed to inflate their life vests but others were pulled down by their heavy loads and drowned. As they got closer to the beach, the assault troops could hear machine-gun rounds striking the steel ramp. All around them the water was being whipped to a froth by bullets and geysers from mortar shells.

The same current that had been lucky at Utah Beach caused a deadly confusion at Omaha. Landing craft came in on the wrong parts of the beach. Units were mixed up, officers were missing, landmarks that the men had studied were not there. With so few paths cleared through the obstacles and minefields, the LCIs drifted back and forth, desperately trying to find a place to land their troops. Navy helmsmen performed feats of heroism to get their passengers ashore through the murderous fire. Some landing craft grounded on uncharted sandbars hundreds of yards from the shore and the men had to wade through deep water or swim with bullets flecking the sea around them. The confusion was almost total.

When the ramps dropped and the assault troops leaped out, the mortar and machine-gun fire grew stronger. Struggling to get ashore through three-foot (.9-m) waves, many were hit and disappeared. The wounded, unable to drag themselves to the beach, drowned in shallow water. Their friends, fighting to survive, could not help them. Those who reached the beach could not advance in the face of the withering fire. They took shelter behind anything that could protect them from the enemy guns. Some crouched behind the still-untouched obstacles, only half-hidden by steel bars and plates. Others flung themselves down on the sand behind the burned-out hulks of the tanks. Still others retreated into the sea and crouched down with only their heads showing above water.

Some men ran for the only shelter they could see: the low, cobblestone seawall. A few made it and huddled behind the wall, unable to move. Many were wounded, weaponless, without officers. It was a shambles.

There were few tanks and fewer heavy guns to return the terrible fire that poured down from the bluffs. For four hours, as more and more assault waves came in, German guns swept the beach and nothing could move. The German commander of the beach defenses sent a triumphant message to his superior at Bayeux, saying that the invasion had been smashed at the water's edge. The German reserves were immediately sent east to attack the British landing points.

On the cruiser *Augusta*, General Omar Bradley reviewed the discouraging reports from Omaha. It was grim reading: losses were high, confusion everywhere, troops unable to advance in the face of the German fire. Unless some miracle happened, Omaha was a failure and the troops, those who

Casualties were heavy on Omaha Beach on D-Day.

survived, would have to be withdrawn and the rest of the landing force put ashore elsewhere.

A failure at Omaha meant that there would be a twenty-mile (32-km) gap open between Utah and the British beaches. It was known that a German panzer division was poised near Caen. If it reached Omaha Beach, it could strike the unprotected flanks of the other Allied landings with disastrous blows. If the landings at Omaha failed, the whole invasion was in great danger.

On the extreme right (the western end) of Omaha Beach, three companies of U.S. Rangers were gallantly assaulting the towering Pointe du Hoc. As usual, plans had gone awry. Their nine landing craft had headed for the wrong place and when a correction had been made it was too late. The follow-up Ranger battalion had not seen the flare that signaled success, and had headed for Omaha to attack the battery of big guns from the land side.

The 225 Rangers reached the base of the cliff and fired rockets with grapnels and rope ladders to the top. Off to sea, two destroyers shelled the cliff top to make the enemy keep his head down. As the Rangers climbed hand over hand up the ropes and ladders, hand grenades and machine-gun fire poured down on them. Here and there, men stiffened, loosened their hold, and toppled down to the bottom of the cliff. Ropes and ladders were cut by the hidden enemy and sent men crashing down, but slowly the Rangers climbed. They cut handholds in the face of the cliff with their knives, fired back as the Germans leaned over the edge with Schmeisser machine pistols, and refused to be thrown back.

Soon the first Rangers reached the top of Pointe du Hoc and threw themselves into the shellholes from the naval bombardment. Under the cover of their fire, more and more soldiers reached the top. As they did, the Germans vanished and the battle was won. There were only ninety unwounded Rangers left of the original 225, but they had won.

When they examined the concrete bunkers, they found

them empty. The big, dangerous guns had never been mounted. There had been no threat to Omaha Beach from the Pointe du Hoc. It had all been for nothing.

For hours the assault troops on Omaha Beach fought to survive under the withering German fire. Not to attack, not to advance, just to live. Stunned and dazed men huddled behind untouched obstacles at the water's edge or under the seawall. Dead and wounded soldiers littered the beach and bodies floated in the surf. The tide was coming in, endangering those wounded men who could not drag themselves out of the water. The horror of the scene had paralyzed the survivors. They could not move in the face of so many enemy guns.

Further landings were halted while General Bradley debated shifting the rest of the landings to the British beaches. Meanwhile the Navy began shelling the German strongpoints again. Destroyers came into the dangerous mined waters to get within range. Rocket ships flung their missiles into the heights behind the beach. To abandon Omaha could lead to disaster. Every risk had to be taken to prevent failure.

Slowly, painfully slowly, the picture began to change. Tanks and heavy guns were brought ashore through the few paths blasted among the obstacles. At once they engaged the German machine-gun and mortar nests. An armored bulldozer smashed a hole in the seawall. One by one the enemy pillboxes were silenced; they could not be replaced by new guns. Unlike the Allies, who could land thousands of men and hundreds of tanks and guns, the Germans were isolated. Allied planes flew low over the roads to the beaches to keep German reinforcements away.

But in the end it was the courage and stubbornness of the individual American soldier that won the day. Inspired by a few officers who walked upright through the worst fire, small groups of infantrymen shook off the paralysis and fear, and began to advance. "They're murdering us here. Let's move

The early success of the Normandy invasion
is captured in this photograph that shows men
and supplies moving off the Omaha beachhead.

inland and get murdered," a colonel shouted. The tough
assistant commander of the 29th Division, Brigadier General
Norman Cota, strode up and down waving his pistol and yelling, "Only two kinds of people are staying on this beach, the
dead and those who are going to die. Now let's get the hell
out of here."

Despite the fire, the barbed wire, and the minefields, the
infantry began to move up the draws, infiltrating between the
remaining enemy pillboxes. The Allied tanks and artillery
could not yet follow them, so the German positions had to be
taken by direct assault by a few determined men. Luckily it
turned out to be easier to hit them from the rear. Soon a few
hundred Allied soldiers were up over the heights and moving inland. One by one the German guns fell silent.

By 1:30 P.M. Bradley had an encouraging report from
Omaha. It said that the troops that had been pinned down
were now advancing on the heights behind the beach. Now
the general had to worry about a counterattack by German
tanks that could sweep his few men back into the sea.

By the end of the day, Omaha Beach was one mile (1.6
km) deep and had cost 2,500 dead, wounded, and missing.

CHAPTER VII

THE
BRITISH
BEACHES

On the left flank of the invasion were the British beaches, stretching from Omaha to the mouth of the Orne River. From west to east they were named Gold, Juno, and Sword, innocent-sounding names never to be forgotten.

This eight-mile-long (13-km) seafront was a well-known resort area before the war, a favorite with British tourists. When the planners for Overlord had made a public appeal for snapshots of the Channel towns of France, thousands of pictures had poured in, showing the cottages, villas, and hotels just back of the beaches, the low dunes, the cleared paths from the water's edge, and a few bluffs dividing the assault area. Now the shallow water was full of concrete-and-steel obstacles with mines attached, barbed wire fences, minefields, and tank traps. The gaily painted houses and hotels were strongpoints, bristling with machine guns and mortars. There were fewer cannon here than at Omaha, but these were well placed to sweep the beaches. The estimate of casualties had been high.

A line of sandbars and reefs just off the beaches meant that the landings would have to take place on an incoming tide. That meant that the first landing craft could not approach until about an hour after the first landings on Utah and Omaha. This would allow the initial bombardment to last

*These British and Canadian troops carried bicycles
as they waded ashore at Normandy.*

two hours, compared to half an hour in the U.S. sector. It was expected that very little German opposition would survive the shelling from the big naval guns.

Everything went off smoothly and on schedule at first. The fleet came in and anchored in the dark, protected by a smoke screen from the German coastal guns at Le Havre off to the left. The landing craft came alongside the transports and the men climbed down the rope ladders in the blackness. The LCTs were lowered into the water and all the landing craft began to circle, waiting for the order to go in.

At first light, the ships began to rake the beaches and the low hills. Clouds of smoke and dust hid the landing sites, and all that could be seen were the red flashes of the exploding shells. Rocket ships moved in close and fired thousands of rockets against any visible target. For two hours the bombardment went on until it seemed that nothing could live under the murderous shelling. But once again the enemy was protected by thick concrete walls and deep bunkers. They waited, deafened by the noise but otherwise barely touched. When the shelling stopped, they quickly came out to man their guns. Again it would be up to the individual soldier, rifleman, tank crews, and engineers, to take the beaches.

Although the transports had anchored eight miles (13 km) out (rather than twelve [19 km]), it was still a long, cold and wet trip for the landing craft. The waters were rough and the men in them thoroughly soaked and seasick. Luckily, the LCT commanders decided not to put their tanks into the choppy water and came within a mile (1.6 km) of the beach, where the sea was calmer and shallower. Even so, several tanks tore their inflatable canvas life belts, filled with water, and quickly sank, but most plowed through the waves and reached the beaches.

The engineers went in first and ran into a storm of enemy fire. From the villas and hotels just across the sandy beaches, machine guns and mortars raked the demolition crews struggling in waist-deep water to set the charges. Because of the high tide, many of the obstacles were hidden, many were uncharted, and there were new minefields. Just as at Omaha, the engineers suffered terrible losses from enemy fire but they stubbornly went about their job blowing the obstacles one by one. Tanks waddled up on the beaches and fired directly at the German strongpoints. Some were hit by shells and started to burn.

H-Hour was 7:30 A.M. and as the landing craft of the first assault wave neared Gold Beach, the smoke began to lift. Several of the LCIs grounded on the reefs a hundred yards (91 m) offshore with shells exploding in the sea around them. The men dived over the sides and swam the rest of the way, holding their weapons above their heads. Here and there a man would be hit and would disappear under the waves. No one could stop to help, for every man had only one aim: get up on the beach and hit the enemy.

On Gold Beach, the resistance was "light." The Germans defending that sector belonged to a mediocre division, many of whom were foreign "volunteers," Poles and Russians, ex-prisoners of war who fought without enthusiasm and surrendered at the first opportunity. Observers came ashore and directed the fire of the big ships on the enemy strongpoints. The tough British soldiers of the 50th Division crossed the sands despite heavy losses and fired into the buildings at point-blank range. Any German position that could not be taken at once was bypassed as the troops rushed up the low hills, through the marshland, and pushed inland almost four miles (6.4 km).

Behind them the buildup went on. More landing craft crashed through the reefs and the obstacles and carried reinforcements onto the sands. Tanks and heavy artillery were unloaded and went immediately into action. Some of the tanks were new inventions: one type had flails in front to beat the ground and set off mines; others carried bridging equipment or logs to allow antitank ditches to be crossed. There were tanks with flamethrowers and still others without

British troops gather on the beach
for the long march inland.

turrets that rammed seawalls so that vehicles could drive right over them.

By nine o'clock, it looked as if the landings had been successful. One by one the German defenses had been taken and, except for light shelling from distant guns, Gold Beach was secure. But the fighting had just begun. The Germans had decided to hold this sector lightly at the waterline, but to increase the resistance as the invaders moved inland. More and more machine-gun and mortar positions opened fire and soon the British soldiers were slowed and stopped at many points. The town of Bayeux—where William the Conqueror is buried—was not taken immediately, nor was contact made with the other beaches. Every Allied soldier had the same worry: when would the Germans counterattack? Could the weak assault force hold off a determined thrust by panzer divisions?

In the middle beach, Juno, the Canadian 3rd Infantry Division came ashore and was met by a withering fire. Landing craft exploded and flung bodies into the sea. Machine guns cut down the first wave as it waded through the surf and mortars blasted the troops as they scrambled up onto the sands. Bodies floated in the surf amid the wreckage of landing craft, vehicles, and supplies. For a while it looked like a disaster, another Omaha, but slowly the picture changed. More and more tanks came ashore and engaged the enemy. Flail tanks beat paths through the minefields and gave protection behind them to the advancing infantry. Luckily, there were few heavy guns, the German trenches close to the water were finally overrun, and later landings were unopposed, but it was heavy going inland. Tough house-to-house fighting went on everywhere and there was a tragic mistake when naval guns shelled their own men.

The Canadians, by sheer heroism, made the greatest advance of D-Day, ripping their way 10 miles (16 km). But still the first-day objectives were not reached.

At the extreme left of the British beaches reaching to the mouth of the Orne River was the most heavily defended sector, Sword. Here the swift incoming tide was treacherous, the underwater obstacles numerous, and the enemy positions well sited to sweep the beach. The naval and air bombardment that preceded the landings again had little effect except to shake up the defenders. The German heavy guns were ready and many were on the far side of the river where they could not be attacked by infantry. Once more it would be a toe-to-toe slugging match between men in well-protected bunkers and the assault troops struggling out of the water.

First of all, Sword Beach was narrow because of extensive mud flats on the left and low hills on the right. That decreased the number of soldiers that could be landed at one time and made the enemy's job easier. When the men of the East Yorkshire Regiment landed on the left flank, they were met with such intense machine-gun and mortar fire that they lost almost a third of their troops getting across the beach. For the first and only time on D-Day, German bombers appeared as twelve Junker-JU-88s dropped bombs on the advancing troops. They had little effect and were quickly driven off.

More and more troops came ashore on the narrow beach to fight their way through the murderous fire. The sands were littered with the wreckage of war. As the amphibious tanks rolled up onto the beach, several burst into flames but the others did heroic work in blasting the enemy positions. Most of the casualties on Sword occurred during the first hour of the assault. Once the invaders penetrated the German strongpoints, the tide of battle turned in their favor.

It was on Sword that the first French troops came ashore to fight on their native soil. Even before the first British troops landed, French marines captured the town of Ouistreham and relieved the beleaguered French airborne troops who had dropped into the town during the night and had suffered heavy losses in the fighting against the German defenders. When the town was secured, the French flag was raised to announce the end of the four-year German occupation.

Eight miles (13 km) inland from Sword was the key town of Caen. It was supposed to have been taken on the first day, but the worn-out British troops could not advance more than three miles (4.8 km). Here they dug in, brought up tanks and antitank guns from the beach, and waited for the inevitable panzer counterattack. Unless they could stop the German tanks, the invasion would fail. If the panzers got through to Sword, they could hit and defeat the Canadians at Juno, and threaten Gold.

Meanwhile, the men of the British 6th Airborne Division were fighting to hold the bridges over the Orne ten miles (16 km) away. Unless relieved soon, they would be overwhelmed. Preceded by the skirling of bagpipes, Lord Lovat's commandos set out to fight their way to the paratroopers and glider troops. They had given their word to the airborne that they would be there by noon and they were men of their word.

At 9:30 A.M. Allied Headquarters announced the beginning of Overlord: "Under the command of General Eisenhower, Allied naval forces, supported by strong air forces, began landing Allied armies this morning on the northern coast of France." By telephone, cable, and radio, reporters sent the momentous news around the world.

It was the middle of the night in the United States so most people did not hear the news until they awoke. Then church bells rang, sirens wailed, and prayers were offered for the sons and fathers fighting in Normandy. Along with the fear was a sense of pride, for no one doubted that this was the first step to victory.

The short announcement said nothing about the progress of the battle. No one outside of Allied headquarters knew how chancy was the toehold in France. Even as the news spread, serious thought was being given to abandoning Omaha Beach, leaving the dead and wounded behind. It would be hours before any good news came from that bloody beachhead.

Meanwhile the German commanders were still trying to make up their minds if the Normandy landings were the real invasion. While some insisted that this was the main effort, others hesitated and looked fearfully at the Pas de Calais. What looked like the movement of Patton's "First U.S. Army Group" toward Dover had been reported. The Germans had no idea that this was a phantom army existing only on paper, one of the most successful deception schemes of the war. They hesitated and waited for more information.

Finally, von Rundstedt decided that even if they were a feint, the Allied landings in Normandy had to be attacked and destroyed. At 5 A.M. he called Berlin and demanded the release of the two panzer divisions that were being held back by Hitler. The Fuehrer was asleep and his staff refused to wake him even for such an important decision. Saying that Normandy was a secondary effort, the German High Command would not release the two panzer divisions at the time. They said they would present the facts to Hitler at his regular morning staff meeting. So the only armored force strong enough to hurl the Allies back into the sea was kept out of the battle during the critical morning hours when the issue hung in the balance. Hitler slept. When he woke it was too late to repel the invasion.

As a field marshal, von Rundstedt had the right to telephone Hitler at any time. This he refused to do despite the vital need for the panzers. He had such contempt for the "Bohemian corporal" that he would not humble himself to beg. Rommel might have gotten to the Fuehrer and obtained the release of the tanks, but no one thought to call Rommel at his home near Ulm, Germany. Strangely enough, no one at Hitler's headquarters knew Rommel was on leave and so close by.

It was ten hours after the first Allied paratrooper dropped into Normandy that Rommel received a telephone call from his chief of staff about the landings. The field marshal recognized immediately that this was the main invasion but for some reason did not leave for France until three hours later. The 500-mile (800-km) trip would take him over nine hours and while the Allies were pouring men and equipment into the beachheads, the man whose skill and energy might have defeated the landings was speeding along the roads, out of touch with his headquarters.

Von Rundstedt did have one last card to play: the 21st Panzer Division just south of Caen. It could have been used to clean out the British airborne on the other side of the Orne River, but it is difficult for tanks to chase paratroopers. However the panzers were within striking distance of Sword Beach. The division was under Rommel's command and while Rommel's chief of staff hesitated, the tanks just sat and waited. Orders came and were immediately canceled. Allied planes strafed the long columns of tanks, forcing them to disperse. When the division was finally ordered to attack the British beaches, it took time to get assembled and moving.

It was late afternoon before the first German tanks moved into Caen. There Allied bombings had filled the streets with rubble and progress was very slow. There were losses as British bombers attacked, but the main force of tanks struggled through the choked streets and into the countryside north of the city. Here they ran into the panic-stricken remnants of the German infantry division that had held the hills over the British beaches. The German panzer commander tried to turn them around but the beaten men fled to safety in Caen.

Unknown to the Germans, the 21st Panzer was headed toward a wide gap in the British lines between Juno and Sword beaches. If they could reach the little town of Luc-sur-Mer on the coast, they could crush the British handily. First, the Germans would have to take possession of two heights that blocked their path. The tank commander split his force, sending thirty-five tanks to capture one hill and twenty-five the other. Sitting on the heights, the tanks could blast anything between themselves and the sea.

But they had waited too long. Already the British had

massed tanks, antitank guns, and artillery on the hills. As the German tanks rumbled through the fields, the British held their fire until the last moment. At point-blank range, the British guns shattered the German formations. In a few minutes, twenty German tanks were burning hulks and the rest hastily retreated to nearby woods. When the British tried to drive them out, they in turn were beaten back. It was a stalemate. The Germans could not reach the gap, and the British could not reach Caen.

As the battle raged for the woods, the Germans saw a demoralizing sight. Overhead, a long line of towplanes—five hundred twin-engine craft, each pulling a large glider—passed over. They were headed for the 6th Airborne area with precious reinforcements. Similar glider trains were flying to the Cotentin with help for the U.S. airborne. For the Germans, cut off by Allied planes and naval gunfire, there was no hope of relief. Every German soldier who fell, every German gun lost, was irreplaceable. The German soldiers fought well but without hope for victory.

When Hitler awoke around 10 A.M., his adjutant told him of the confused reports of landings in Normandy. The Fuehrer ordered a staff meeting of all the senior commanders to evaluate the situation. Hitler himself had warned in April that a secondary landing might be made in Normandy to draw troops from the Pas de Calais. At the staff meeting, he found his experts eager to agree with him (it was never safe to argue with the Fuehrer's "military genius"). He ordered an intelligence study made of the ability of the Allies to land in two places, then went off to lunch with a visitor.

The best brains of the German army hastily reviewed their thinking on the invasion and were fooled by Patton's phantom army. They told Hitler that Normandy was a feint and should be cleaned up without too much trouble, and that the powerful German 15th Army, its tanks and reserves, should not be moved from the Pas de Calais. Hitler agreed but ordered the release of the two panzer divisions von

Rundstedt had requested. This, he figured, would be enough to destroy the Allied landings in Normandy.

By the time the message releasing the panzers arrived in France, it was almost 5 P.M. It was too late for the two armored divisions to reach the battle area that day, so they were ordered to attack at first light. With the Allied troops still struggling to hold on, with the beaches still separated by miles, von Rundstedt was optimistic that he would sweep the invaders into the sea. But he underestimated the ability of the Allied air forces to keep panzer columns from using the roads. For forty-eight critical hours, the two panzer divisions struggled to reach the coast under constant strafing.

When they arrived, it was too late. By June 8, the Allied beachhead was one solid, continuous line from Utah to Sword. It was not deep but it was strong. Into this small area over 155,000 soldiers with all their equipment, tanks, artillery, and supplies had been poured on the first day alone. And overhead and offshore, planes and ships guarded the armies of liberation.

CHAPTER VIII

THE
BREAKOUT

In the first twenty-four hours of the invasion, the Allied armies had gained a weak toehold on Hitler's "Fortress Europe." Now it would be a race to determine how fast the Allies could pour men and guns into their beachhead and how fast the Germans could bring up troops to drive out the invaders.

The Allies had serious problems. The gaps between the five beaches had not been closed. The airborne troops were still widely scattered and, most important of all, Caen had not been captured. Here the Germans had concentrated most of their force and were resisting fiercely. (Caen would not fall until mid-July).

The struggle to join and expand the beachheads was a slow, costly business. The hedgerows were natural breastworks and fields had to be captured one by one. Finally, an American sergeant welded two sharpened pieces of metal to the front of a Sherman tank and found that it could rip out part of a hedgerow. This solved one problem, but there were many others.

On the second day, the artificial harbors—the "Mulberries"—were towed into place and sunk. Until a port could be captured, all supplies would have to come over the beaches and the Channel weather was notoriously treacherous. All went well for two weeks, then the worst storm in fifty years

The "Mulberry," a prefabricated port,
was an incredible feat of engineering.

*In the weeks after D-Day, troops continued
to pour into Normandy to reinforce the
Allied forces fighting on the front line.*

hit Normandy. The Mulberry off Omaha was smashed beyond repair. Over three hundred ships of all sizes were thrown up on the beaches. It was a severe setback that could have been a catastrophe except for the capture of Cherbourg a week later.

So slow was the expansion of the beachhead that it took the Allies fifty days to reach the line they should have reached five days after the landings. Still, they were firmly lodged on the French coast and, despite the storm, the build-up was continuing feverishly. By July 2, a million men had landed in France and it was time to break out for the final battle.

The breakout was called "Operation Cobra" and it began on July 25. While Montgomery's army held the major German forces near Caen, Bradley's troops would break through at St.-Lô. The breakout would be preceded by a massive saturation bombing of the German front lines. Thousands of heavy bombers would pulverize the area to open the gate for two U.S. armies.

The day before Cobra began, Hitler ordered the German 15th Army to the Normandy battle area; by now it was clear that there would be no landing at Calais. However, the order was too late. The few divisions of the 15th Army that did arrive in Normandy got there in time to be destroyed.

The saturation bombing was not as successful as it might have been, but the Germans were badly shaken and stunned. When the first American tanks rumbled through the smoke, the defenders fled. Right behind General Courtney H. Hodges's 1st Army came the new 3rd Army led by General Patton. The phantom 1st Army Group had served its purpose and Patton was now leading a real army.

On August 7, the Germans launched a strong counterattack, using the men and tanks that had been fighting at Caen. Their objective was to reach the town of Mortain and strike the advancing Americans in the flank. The counterattack failed and was turned into a rout. Patton and Hodges struck from the south while Montgomery pushed down from the north. Between them they squeezed the Germans into a bag. Trying to break out, the enemy had to run a terrible gauntlet of fire from the ground and from the air. Few escaped the slaughter along the roads back to Falaise. The breakout of the Allied armies from the Normandy beachhead would now be almost unopposed.

On August 15, two Allied armies—one American and one French—landed in the south of France not far from Nice. After sweeping aside light German resistance, they captured the major seaports of Toulon and Marseilles, threatened the German rear in northern Italy, and drove north up the Rhône Valley to join the Allied armies that had broken out of the Normandy beachhead. Then, on a broad front, the Allies began the drive toward Germany.

After a wild pursuit that drove the broken German armies out of France and Belgium, the Allies were brought to a halt at the Belgian–Dutch border. Their supply lines from the Normandy beaches had been stretched too thin, Cherbourg was still not in full operation, and besieged Germans still held the other Channel ports. In an attempt to break through the stiffening German resistance in Holland, three Allied airborne divisions were dropped behind the enemy lines as the British ground troops attacked. It was a gallant try but it failed. The critical bridge across the Rhine at Arnhem could not be taken by the British 1st Airborne Division, which lost three quarters of its soldiers before retreating.

In the middle of December, the Germans counterattacked in the hilly Ardennes region of Belgium (the Battle of the Bulge). Hitler's aim was to split the Allied armies by capturing Antwerp, thus forcing the surrounded English troops into another Dunkirk. The offensive failed after an initial success against the surprised U.S. divisions. This was Hitler's last throw of the dice, his last try to stave off defeat. It was also another mistake, for the German losses in the battle left them too weak to keep the Allies from crossing the Rhine into Germany.

But it took almost three months of heavy fighting before

the Rhine was reached. In March 1945, both Patton and Montgomery fought their way across the Rhine into Germany at two different points. After that it was another mad pursuit of the broken enemy who, having lost hope of victory, surrendered by the thousands.

The Soviet armies had smashed through the German lines in the east and, surrounding Berlin, were rushing westward to meet the advancing Allies. The meeting took place at the Elbe River on April 25. Now events moved at a quickening pace.

Rather than be taken prisoner and tried as a war criminal, Adolf Hitler, leader of a Nazi Germany that he had boasted would last a thousand years, committed suicide. He shot the mistress he had just married and himself while hiding in a bunker deep under the ruins of Berlin.

On May 2, Berlin fell to the Soviet armies after a bloody struggle in the shattered city.

On May 7, at Allied headquarters in Reims, France, the Germans surrendered without conditions to General Eisenhower. The war in Europe was over. Operation Overlord had reached a successful conclusion.

D-Day—June 6, 1944—had been the beginning of the end of Nazi Germany. The thousand-year regime had lasted twelve years.

How many men died in the first twenty-four hours of the assault on the Normandy beaches? Such figures are hard to come by because of the confused fighting. Total Allied casualties—dead, wounded, and missing—are estimated to be between ten and twelve thousand. The Germans are silent on their losses.

Today there are still signs of D-Day along the Channel coast. The massive German gun emplacements still look grimly down on the beaches. Rusting hulks of the ships sunk to make the artificial harbors still rest in the sea. But most of all it is the military cemeteries with their carefully arranged rows of white crosses and Stars of David that remind the visitors of the cost of the battle.

FOR FURTHER READING

Bradley, General Omar N. *A Soldier's Story*. New York: Holt, Rinehart and Winston, 1951.

Crookenden, Napier. *Drop Zone Normandy*. London: Ian Allan, 1976.

Eisenhower, General Dwight D. *Crusade in Europe*. New York: Doubleday, 1948.

Howarth, David. *D-Day, the Sixth of June, 1944*. New York: McGraw-Hill, 1959.

Marrin, Albert. *Overlord, D-Day and the Invasion of Europe*. New York: Atheneum, 1982.

Paine, Lauran. *D-Day*. London: Robert Hale, 1981.

Ridgway, General Matthew B. *Soldier*. New York: Harper, 1956.

Ryan, Cornelius. *The Longest Day, June 6, 1944*. New York: Simon and Schuster, 1959.

Shulman, Milton. *Defeat in the West*. London: Mercury, 1947.

Taylor, General Maxwell D. *Swords and Plowshares*. New York: W.W. Norton and Sons, 1972.

Tute, W., Costello, J., and Hughes, T. *D-Day*. London: Sidgwick and Jackson, 1974.

INDEX